This book is practical, passionate and b[...]
anyone in leadership at a local church. [...]
outlined in this book could seriously cha[...]
Lyndon Bowring, Executive Chairman of CARE

Identifying and encouraging emerging leaders is one of the most important tasks for Christian leadership. Ignore it and you not only fail to secure the legacy of your own ministry – you miss the opportunity of following in the footsteps of Jesus the Leader, who chose twelve people and then invested everything in their lives. I know Marcus and have seen at first-hand the immense fruitfulness of his vision for equipping grace-filled leaders. His urgent plea to value leadership training says it all.
David Coffey, Global Ambassador, BMS World Mission and Past President of the Baptist World Alliance

Fruitful Leaders rings with the passion of a disciple who loves God, his gospel and his people. Marcus insists that the most fundamental quality needed in authentic spiritual leadership is a constantly refreshed love relationship with the Lord, bubbling up into joy and worship. He tackles honestly the challenges to that, and offers practical, compassionate wisdom on how to deal with them. He urges churches to invest deeply in developing a new generation of godly leaders, an acute need throughout the global church, as well as in caring for current leaders. And by the way, Marcus models with integrity what he writes about. Read this book – and buy copies for your church leaders too.
Rose Dowsett, OMF International, Vice-Chair of the World Evangelical Alliance Mission Commission

Among the many titles on this subject, *Fruitful Leaders* has a refreshing simplicity and directness. But don't be fooled. The ideas here are radical as well as utterly biblical and practical: growing leaders of all kinds *within* the local church; defining leaders in terms of their *spiritual life* and their enjoyment of God and his grace; nurturing leaders who *love* those whom they serve; and supporting leaders so that they *flourish* rather than burn out.

Given the growing leadership crisis across the churches, this book provides a refreshing and realistic agenda for healthy and productive change in churches large and small. Here's an approach that will release many more people into effective Christian ministry of all kinds: I highly commend it.
Jonathan Lamb, Director of Langham Preaching, Langham Partnership International, and Chairman of the Keswick Convention

As timely as it is wise; as practical as it is focused; as convicting as it is scriptural. Marcus's book should be read and acted upon by all those who love the local church, whether leaders or not.
Adrian Reynolds, Director of Ministry, The Proclamation Trust

Marcus has long had a passion to see the church led by truly spiritual leaders, growing in their knowledge and love for God, deeply rooted in his Word, captivated by his grace and filled with joy in Christ. This book is an impassioned call to the church to recognize the urgent need to grow vibrant leaders like this.

In a punchy, readable style Marcus combines incisive biblical exposition with anecdote, empirical evidence, practical guidance, pastoral wisdom, and opportunities for personal reflection and self-assessment. He speaks to everyone – leaders, trainers, aspiring leaders, congregation members – encouraging and challenging us all to make the development and support of spiritual leaders a high priority. If every congregation were captivated by the author's infectious passion for God and his glory, the church would be better able to identify and deploy the gifted people Christ has given to it. The cause of the gospel would be strengthened, as people are prepared to do the works of service that build up the body.
John Stevens, Director, Fellowship of Independent Evangelical Churches

Feel blunt as a leader? Unsure of your mission? Are dullness or weakness creeping in? Marcus's book will serve as a bracing refreshment and a warm encouragement, strengthening your soul and sharpening your vision.
Simon Virgo, Lead Elder, King's Church Kingston, Newfrontiers

fruitful leaders
how to make, grow,
             love and keep them

Marcus Honeysett

fruitful leaders
how to make, grow, love and keep them

ivp

Living Leadership

INTER-VARSITY PRESS
Norton Street, Nottingham NG7 3HR, England
Email: ivp@ivpbooks.com
Website: www.ivpbooks.com

© Marcus Honeysett, 2011

Marcus Honeysett has asserted his right under the Copyright, Designs and Patents Act, 1988, to be identified as Author of this work.

All rights reserved. No part of this publication may be reproduced, stored in a retrieval system, or transmitted, in any form or by any means, electronic, mechanical, photocopying, recording or otherwise, without the prior permission of the publisher or the Copyright Licensing Agency.

Unless otherwise stated, Scripture quotations are taken from the Holy Bible, New International Version. Copyright © 1973, 1978, 1984 by International Bible Society. Used by permission of Hodder & Stoughton, a division of Hodder Headline Ltd. All rights reserved. 'NIV' is a trademark of International Bible Society. UK trademark number 1448790.

First published 2011

British Library Cataloguing in Publication Data
A catalogue record for this book is available from the British Library.

ISBN: 978–1–84474–544–9

Set in Dante 12/15pt
Typeset in Great Britain by CRB Associates, Potterhanworth, Lincolnshire
Printed and bound in Great Britain by MPG Books Ltd, Bodmin, Cornwall

Inter-Varsity Press publishes Christian books that are true to the Bible and that communicate the gospel, develop discipleship and strengthen the church for its mission in the world.

Inter-Varsity Press is closely linked with the Universities and Colleges Christian Fellowship, a student movement connecting Christian Unions in universities and colleges throughout Great Britain, and a member movement of the International Fellowship of Evangelical Students. Website: www.uccf.org.uk

For our support team:
Chris and Jo, Philip and Margaret,
Mark and Josie and Graham
– precious friends and partners in the gospel

CONTENTS

	Acknowledgments	13
	Section 1: I will build my church	
1.	God loves your church	17
2.	What is spiritual leadership?	27
	Section 2: How to grow vibrant leaders in your church	
3.	Clear, dig and nurture	47
4.	Developing yourself as a spiritual leader	63
5.	Leaders who love the Holy Spirit and the Bible	81
6.	Caring for yourself as a leader	97
7.	You could be a leader-maker	107
	Section 3: How to look after your leaders	
8.	Look out – There's a cliff!	125
9.	How to love and encourage spiritual leaders	141
10.	Let your leaders lead	161
	Conclusion: Spiritual leadership to the glory of God	173
	Afterword: A vision for lifelong learning	183

Appendix 1: Growing in God –
Spiritual review questions   189

Appendix 2: Growing in leadership –
Practical review exercise   193

Appendix 3: Elements to include in a
leader-training course in your church   195

Appendix 4: Leadership-killers   201

Further reading   205

What is Living Leadership?   207

Notes   211

ACKNOWLEDGMENTS

The material in this book has taken shape over many years in a wide variety of churches and missions who have invited me to speak or deliver training on leadership. The Universities and Colleges Christian Fellowship London staff team deserve special mention for being the test bed in which so many ideas about leadership were tried out. More recently, it has been a wonderful and humbling experience to serve with the trustees and strategy team of Living Leadership. They have not only brought an exciting new ministry into being but have allowed me the time to write this book. Finally, it is a pleasure to serve alongside leaders of skill, passion and love on the leadership team of Crofton Baptist Church.

I was privileged during the summer of 2010 to be invited to take the School of Leadership at the annual Keswick Convention in the Lake District. Large portions of chapters 2, 4, 6 and 7 are drawn from those seminars.

Thanks to Tim Chester for contributing the thought-provoking afterword and to Eleanor Trotter at IVP for her brilliant editing and encouragement.

Special thanks to James and Martha Sercombe, and Brendan and Sandra Caldwell and their families for inviting me to their homes to write. This book wouldn't have happened without you.

SECTION 1:
I will build my church

1. GOD LOVES YOUR CHURCH

Main principle: God wants to build up your local church, and he provides gifts of spiritual leadership to help the flock grow

---

Communities of Christians come in many shapes, sizes and flavours. God is using large and small churches, multicultural and monocultural churches, churches with lively worship styles that appeal to the young, and churches that prefer solid older hymns, to witness to neighbourhoods and to the world. Bible-believing churches may exhibit many surface differences, but one thing is true of them all: God *loves* local churches. He wants to see them built up and flourishing.

Local churches are God's idea, not human institutions. The Bible describes them as the household of God. It says that God lives in the middle of these communities of disciples, through the Holy Spirit (Ephesians 2:22). Jesus revealed just how important churches are to God. He promised God's spiritual provision and protection as we participate in God's plans and purposes when he said, 'I will build my church, and the gates of hell will not overcome it' (Matthew 16:18).

Jesus is committed to building his church around the world. And in case you are still in any doubt about how valuable churches are to God, he says in Ephesians 1 that he has made Jesus head over everything in the whole universe *for the church*. Just imagine that – Jesus is exerting his ruling power in heaven for the good of your church here on earth. Maybe you are part of a church where this reality feels a long way from your current experience, but that doesn't mean it isn't true. God wants your church to thrive. That might not mean spectacular growth in numbers, but it will mean all the believers knowing and enjoying God and falling deeper and deeper in love with Jesus Christ.

God wants to use your church

Your church is a team invited by God to work with him to fulfil his great purposes in the world. If you had to sum up God's purposes in a single sentence, what would you say? I believe the Bible's answer would go something like: *God's purpose is that the whole world will see his greatness and glory. He wants the good news of his grace to be received and rejoiced in by all people, everywhere.*

The apostle Paul says three times in Ephesians 1 that the whole purpose of our lives, and the reason God calls people to belong to him, is 'for the praise of his glory', or 'to the praise of his glorious grace'. Did you realize that is what your life is for? Or that it is what your church is for? Sadly, churches sometimes forget who they are and swap a passion for this great purpose of God for some other vision or favourite activity. But the apostle is clear that God's vision for the church is that 'the manifold wisdom of God should be made known to the rulers and authorities in the heavenly realms, according to his eternal purpose' (Ephesians 3:10–11). If you have got into the habit of thinking that church is dull, then God is telling you through Ephesians that it is time to wake up to the true identity of the church and get involved in his earth-shattering plans! As it says in 1 Peter 2: 'But you are a chosen people, a royal priesthood, a holy nation, a people belonging to God, that you may declare the praises [i.e. to the world, not just singing praise in church] of him who called you out of darkness into his wonderful light' (1 Peter 2:9).

What is a local church?

The best short statement about what churches are for is the Great Commission. Here Jesus told his disciples to 'go and make disciples of all nations, baptising them in the name of the Father and of the Son and of the Holy Spirit, and teaching them to obey everything I have commanded you' (Matthew 28:19–20). In his version, Luke adds a couple of details about what is involved in making disciples: preaching repentance and forgiveness of sins in Jesus' name to all nations (Luke 24:47).

Local churches are communities for making mature disciples, people who follow Jesus more and more closely and participate actively in the Matthew 28 purpose of the church. Disciples seek God for his grace each day of their lives, experiencing his love, loving his Word and enjoying being his worshipping people. They tell everyone else how amazing he is. This should be the focus of all church activities. It is the purpose of outreach, community and compassion ministries. The core purpose of communities of disciples is to make more and more disciples, so that God is worshipped and his grace is received and enjoyed by all people everywhere.

Churches don't exist to run comfortable clubs and social activities. We exist to impact the world with the good news of God's grace.

Gifts from God

God gives all kinds of gifts and abilities to followers of Jesus to enable churches to participate in his purposes. All Christians have some spiritual gifts to use, whether or not they have yet discovered what these are. Grace-gifts for building up the church include wisdom, knowledge, faith, healing, miracles, prophecy, distinguishing between spirits, tongues and their interpretation, the ability to help others, administration, serving, teaching, encouraging, contributing to others' needs, leadership and mercy (Romans 12:6–8 and 1 Corinthians 12:8–11, 28–29).

This book is specifically about gifts of spiritual leadership. It is essential that every gift from God is harnessed and used to extend his kingdom. Nobody's spiritual gifts should be overlooked or underused. Those with the gift of leadership have particular responsibility for building up the body of Christ to maturity and for releasing everyone else's gifts for service.

In Ephesians 4 Paul says that God gives a variety of leadership gifts and ministries to the church 'to prepare God's people for works of service, so that the body of Christ may be built up until we all reach unity in the faith and in the knowledge of the Son of God and become mature, attaining to the whole measure of the fulness of Christ' (Ephesians 4:12–13).

There are lots of different types of leadership roles in the Bible. Leadership isn't just limited to the pastor, priest or vicar. There were spirit-filled servants appointed for practical tasks, elders directing the spiritual and strategic vision of local churches, apostles, prophets, evangelists and pastor-teachers.

We see this variety mirrored in churches today with Sunday school and home group leaders, paid ministers and unpaid ones, preachers and carers, elders and PCC members, lay readers and service leaders, outreach leaders and finance team leaders, all exercising the gift of spiritual leadership in some way. Leadership will look different in each of these areas, but every spiritual leader will have the same aim: to shape and equip the community of disciples so that people know God, become more and more like Jesus and actively participate in God's plans.

Growing spiritual leaders in your church

I believe passionately that God wants to raise up spiritual leaders in and through our local churches – and not just paid full-timers either. The biblical picture is of a vibrant culture of leadership across the breadth of church life, with different kinds of leaders in different areas and activities.

The modern idea of a congregation with a single leader who does everything, while everyone else passively receives what he provides, is unknown in the Bible. Moreover, it causes churches to expect that God will give us only a very few, highly trained élite leaders, often brought in from outside. Speaking from the perspective of UK churches, the majority sadly often don't expect God to raise up leaders from within, even though this is the normal, biblical pattern (but this is far from being just a British issue). 'Wherever leaders come from, it isn't here' is a common mindset. I often come across churches who think they should send the occasional person to theological college and then buy leadership back in, fully formed, thereby avoiding the pain of new leaders making mistakes. Elsewhere, the lack of vision for training leaders within the congregation leads to people being asked to take on leadership roles, but without any nurture to help them grow in leadership. The fact is that the majority of churches have no regular, ongoing leadership training programme or strategy. I believe this lack is crippling many churches. They don't expect God to raise up leaders from within and therefore don't devote time, energy, money or manpower to nurture and train them if he does.

I don't know how to start: Karen's story

Karen has been a stay-at-home mum, but now that her kids have gone off to school she wants to use her increased free time to serve in the church. The church wants to get a daytime fellowship group going, and the minister thinks that Karen would be just the person to lead it. However, Karen hasn't ever taken responsibility for developing a group and hasn't had much experience leading a Bible study or doing pastoral work.

'Don't worry,' the minister tells her. 'You'll be fine. There really isn't much to it; it's not difficult. Just have a go! I'm sure you'll pick it up as you go along.'

'What's actually involved?' Karen asks.

'Whatever you like, really,' comes the reply. 'Just get something off the ground. Anything will be a step up from where we are now.'

'What training will I get? And how will I know whether I'm doing the right things?' Karen asks. 'Will anyone keep an eye on the group and let me know if they think anything is going wrong?'

'There isn't anyone with the time or space to do that, I'm afraid. But I can let you have a few books that will help you pick up some basic skills. You've been in a home group before so you've seen what can be done. If you feel you're getting out of your depth, then my door is always open,' says the minister.

> **To consider:**
>
> - What help would it be reasonable for Karen to expect so that she can do a good job?
> - What would prevent her from getting it?
> - Should she agree to take on this commitment or not? Explain your answer.

Karen's story is fictitious – but not *very* fictitious. Most churches don't provide such help as a matter of course. It therefore becomes much more difficult for Karen to explore whether she should take on the job, or whether God is giving her the necessary gifts and abilities.

How to encourage Karen – The vision of this book

I nearly called this book *Encouraging Karen*, but then I thought that nobody would know what it was about! This is a book for everyone. God wants to raise up leaders *in your church, for your church*, and if you aren't one of them already, maybe you could be. This is a book for Karen and lots of others like her. This book is for you if you ever:

- Wonder if God might be giving you spiritual gifts for leadership
- Feel like you would love to have a go at leading in some aspect of church life but would never know where to start
- Ask yourself how to help your current leaders in the joys and struggles of leadership

- Long to see a vibrant culture of leadership nurturing and releasing the gifts of every believer
- Pray that God would raise up new leaders in your church

Churches need to pray and plan together as a whole about how to encourage their 'Karens'. Every church needs to figure out how to energize its current leaders and then liberate them to bring on the next generation of leaders. Every church needs to nurture its existing leaders so that they flourish and continue to grow rather than wither and burn out under the stresses and strains of leadership. Leadership must be nurtured in every aspect of church life.

My aim is to set out a threefold vision:

1. We have an urgent need for many Christ-glorifying biblical leaders in all aspects of church life. Churches should expect God to equip and give gifts of leadership to people within their fellowship because he loves the church.
2. The major responsibility for ensuring that all kinds of local leaders are developed, released, sustained and nurtured belongs within the local church. Every congregation should make it a priority to give existing leaders the time and resources to disciple new or junior leaders. No church should think that this is someone else's job or that the responsibility can be simply handed over to Bible schools or training conferences.
3. We need to nurture and sustain leaders in our churches for the whole duration of their leadership, so that they grow in leading and find the task a constant delight rather than a burden. We need to help them grow as Christians as well as in leading. We must care

for their personal walk with God as well as their leadership skills. This is as much a need for a long-serving, full-time minister as it is for a new home group leader.

Identify, encourage, resource and support

If you aren't currently seeing God giving new leaders and gifts of leadership in your church, don't panic! You are far from alone. In fact you are in the majority. But the very fact that you are in the majority reveals that something is wrong in lots of churches. When we don't see enough new leaders coming through, or those like Karen are unable to get the help they need to flourish, it is simply because of man-made hindrances and hurdles. It isn't God being stingy with gifts! He loves the church. He will never give up on her. He is preparing her as a pure, spotless bride for his Son, radiant and beautiful. He is committed to providing everything she needs to be built up and perfected.

We're going to see what we can do in our churches to identify and remove these hurdles. The health and growth of every church depends on having leaders who build up the flock to maturity and who are bold under fire from the world and the devil. In turn, having vibrant leaders is a consequence of how well local churches identify, encourage, resource and support them.

Please pray as you read this book that God will give wisdom to your church about how to develop a passion for growing godly leaders. There could be a lot of value in reading this book with others, and the questions work well in group discussion as well as in personal reflection. Full-time leaders will find this a useful book to read with home group leaders, deacons or PCC members.

Pause now and pray that God will make you a keen encourager with a deep desire to help the current generation of leaders – and the following one too – to lead boldly for Christ: building up the church, equipping every Christian for service and witness, and proclaiming the gospel message courageously and daringly.

> **To consider:**
>
> - If you asked a cross-section of ordinary people in your church, 'What is the purpose of our church?' how do you think they would respond? (Try this out!)
> - Complete the following statement: The job of leaders in our church is to . . .
>   Explain your answer.
> - Do you really expect God to provide home-grown leaders in your church? If not, why not?

2. WHAT IS SPIRITUAL LEADERSHIP?

Main principle: The work of spiritual leaders is to serve other people in love, so that God receives glory

Being run ragged: John's story

John is a twenty-nine-year-old vicar. He has been leading a church for a year, and to be honest it has been a depressing and confusing time. One evening he confides to you that he is feeling heavily burdened and stressed by the mass of demands he feels obliged to meet.

'You would be amazed at what people think their vicar ought to be able to do,' he says. 'It's like I am meant to be Superman. Let me give you some examples.

'The young people want me to be a worship leader, and the old people want me to spend all day doing pastoral visits. And lots of people just want their favourite activities to run effectively. And the home group leaders want a theological educator and a skills coach.

'A large percentage of the congregation want someone who does everything for them while they just receive and consume what I provide. The business people want me to be a professional strategist and keep telling me how effective management is done in the "real world". People with evangelistic gifts are upset because I'm not great at first-contact door-to-door work.

'Some people think I'm employed to do special parts of Sunday services that only élite, ordained leaders can do. And everyone expects me never to struggle with sin. I feel like I am meant to be all-competent and all-gifted, demonstrate every talent to a high degree, be all things to every group in the church, never reveal any of my struggles – and have perfectly behaved children into the bargain.'

'So what do *you* think is the most important part of being a Christian leader?' you ask.

'I just don't know any more,' John replies. 'Nobody is giving me much guidance, but if I can't decide what the heart of the job is, how can I decide what to say "yes" or "no" to? I feel like I'm being pulled in every direction but not managing to please anybody.'

To consider:

- What do you think is the core of Christian leadership?
- What are the possible dangers for John if his situation continues unchanged?
- Is John likely to grow other leaders? Why or why not?
- What advice would you give him?

Competing demands

There are a lot of books and conferences about leadership, many of which – both Christian and non-Christian – provide valuable insights. However, even among Christian writers, definitions of what leadership actually *is* vary considerably. I have come across all those John mentions above and many others, including:

- A position in an organizational structure like a CEO (pastor) or middle manager (home group leader)
- The élite, trained professional
- The theological educator
- The vision-caster who raises aspirations and expectations
- The sole preacher
- The model character
- The person employed to make good things happen

It seems that everyone has different ideas of what leaders should be and what leaders should do for them.

Leadership of a different kind

So far I have resisted defining spiritual leadership, but it is time now to nail it down. This definition is true for every kind of Christian leader, equally relevant to Sunday school teachers as it is to vicars, to youth leaders as to elders.

Here is how the apostle Paul describes the work of leadership: 'What, after all, is Apollos? And what is Paul? Only servants, through whom you came to believe' (1 Corinthians 3:5), and 'We . . . preach . . . Jesus Christ as Lord, and ourselves as your servants for Jesus' sake' (2 Corinthians 4:5).

Paul tells us what spiritual leadership is: servanthood among God's people. But just as importantly, he tells us what the goal of servant leadership is: it is *for Jesus' sake*. In other words, so that Jesus receives glory in other people's lives as they learn to trust, follow and obey him. Serving people in this way certainly doesn't mean just doing whatever they want us to do.

Biblical leadership in the church is different from all other kinds of leadership. Elsewhere the goal is strategies, plans and initiatives for organizational growth, whereas the goal of spiritual leadership is God being glorified in lives that are yielded to him. Strategy, vision, communication and management are important too, but they aren't the most important things because they don't, in themselves, build spiritual value in lives.

A church is a team, a community with a purpose. The goal of the team is that God receives glory. The purpose of spiritual leadership is to serve the team by leading it towards the goal: becoming the people God wants them to be and doing the things God wants them to do.

For Jesus' sake: Taking others into the purposes of God

Paul says of his own leadership that he labours with God's energy to present everyone mature in Christ, by proclaiming Jesus, admonishing and teaching with all wisdom. His purpose as a leader is that they may know 'Christ in [them], the hope of glory' (Colossians 1:27–28).

God gives leaders to churches to help them *be* something and *do* something:

- They help others bring God glory through having their priorities, ambitions and goals changed by the good

news. Leaders help people put God's glory at the heart of all their decisions.
- They help others participate in God's purposes by being involved in local and global activities that bring him glory, whether through evangelism, compassion ministries or becoming vibrant witnesses in the workplace.

People look to leaders to see and hear about God's purposes and discover how they too can be involved with God. Serving the church for the sake of the Lord means that every aspect of leadership is done so that God is exalted in the life of every disciple, in order that he is more widely known and praised around the world. Leaders serve in order that Christ is formed in people's hearts by faith and in order that non-Christians are invited to commit their lives to God. That is what is wrapped up in that little phrase: 'for Jesus' sake'.

The foundation for discipleship – Enjoying God

Paul loved the church in Philippi. When he wrote to them from prison, he said that his dearest desire was to be with them, and that if God released him he would work with them 'for your progress and joy in the faith, so that through my being with you again your joy in Jesus Christ will overflow on account of me' (Philippians 1:25–26).

What an amazing definition of spiritual leadership: working with people for their progress and joy in God, because you want churches and believers to overflow with happiness in Jesus Christ! This is why every church should love having spiritual leaders. Churches should be devastated when there are none around, and pray eagerly for God to provide them. It is tragic when churches abuse godly leaders or dig in their heels and refuse to follow them. This is a sure way to church stagnation and for people no longer to overflow with joy in Jesus.

Philippi wasn't an isolated example either. Paul says to the Corinthians, 'Not that we lord it over your faith, but we work with you for your joy, because it is by faith you stand firm' (2 Corinthians 1:24). This is amazing. Paul thinks that we grow in firm faith when we are enjoying God. Therefore the work of spiritual leaders is to help people enjoy God, knowing that increasing faith will be the result.

Foundational principles for joy

When I see leaders who are clearly on fire to help people know and enjoy God, delight in his Word and love being part of his purposes, I always try to discern the foundational principles of their leadership. What makes them lead the way they do? Which parts of the Bible do they look to in order to learn how to be good and godly leaders?

Here are seven foundations that I often see in the leaders I most respect and want to follow:

1. They believe that God's greatest concern is that the glory of his grace is proclaimed and known and praised. As it says in Ephesians 1, our lives are for the praise of God's glory. Leaders who believe that God created the universe so that he receives worship will mould every aspect of church life accordingly.
2. They understand that the heart of leadership is to serve the church for the sake of Christ, i.e. so that Jesus is made much of. Such leaders don't get sidetracked into merely leading popular and comfortable activities that distract from this core purpose.

3. They are likely to be enjoying the work of the Holy Spirit in their lives. The Bible says that leadership is a gift from the Holy Spirit to build up the church (Romans 12:8). We can see this in action in 1 Corinthians 2:4–5: 'My message and my preaching were not with wise and persuasive words, but with a demonstration of the Spirit's power, so that your faith might not rest on men's wisdom, but on God's power.'

   The power of the Holy Spirit is manifested through the centrality of the message about the cross of Jesus. In a similar verse Paul says that his words didn't come with human wisdom 'lest the cross of Christ be emptied of its power' (1 Corinthians 1:17). Acts 20:28 also teaches that leadership is based on the foundation of the cross: 'Keep watch over yourselves and all the flock of which the Holy Spirit has made you overseers. Be shepherds of the church of God, which he bought with his own blood.'
4. They have a clear understanding that the purpose of a church is to go and make disciples by declaring the greatness and wonder of God to the world. If this is the purpose of the church, then it is also the purpose of leaders: to make and shape a community of disciples to make even more disciples.
5. They know that a church grows into this purpose when individually all the disciples are becoming spiritually mature. Ephesians 4:12–13 says that leaders are given by God 'to prepare [his] people for works of service, so that the body of Christ may be built up . . . and become mature'. This involves helping them know and understand about God, in order that they can adore, enjoy, worship and follow him.
6. They are inevitably people who themselves want to grow in Christlike character. Many of the epistles teach that the character of Christ is essential to spiritual

leaders: personal prayer and worship life, for example, are vitally important. The Bible couldn't be clearer that the attitude of leaders is more important than their skills, and that their love is more important than their activities. The most important thing of all is the display of God's glory in their characters.

The older I get, the more I want to ask all leaders, 'What is your worship and prayer life like?' That is the way to see if God has their heart. Worshipful, prayerful leaders live by faith, not by sight. They are teachable by God because their hearts are happy in him.

7. They know that God gives gifts to all his people for ministry, and that their role is to equip all believers. The people who do the work of God are all the people of God, not just an élite few. Leaders have a particular role to play in releasing the contribution of everyone else. And those who can't or won't release the gifts and ministries that God has given others are hindering rather than helping the church.

So biblical leadership is based on these principles:

- The purposes of God
- The worship of God and Jesus Christ
- The work of the Holy Spirit
- The mission of the worldwide church
- The centrality of growing mature disciples
- The development of Christlike character in the leader
- The need to release and facilitate the gifts of every disciple in the church

If we miss some of these elements out, then our understanding of the church and leadership is deformed. For example, if we *only* emphasize the parts about character and discipleship, we will develop a caring, pastoral understanding of leadership, but miss out mission. Even more importantly, if we miss out the first two points, leadership quickly becomes disconnected from God's foundational purposes and no longer leads people to enjoy God, worship him or participate with him in his great plans.

> **To consider:**
>
> Pause for a moment to answer this question: what does a person exercising spiritual leadership look like? Think about your own leadership, or that of a leader you admire.

What do spiritual leaders look like?

I hope after reading thus far that you didn't start by listing activities. The job of leaders is not *mainly* to put on Sunday services or run home groups, although it may involve that. At root it isn't to pastor people through hardship either, although it will involve that too.

I hope you didn't talk about organizational position or status either. The disciples James and John went to Jesus and asked, 'Can we sit on your right and left hand when you become king?' Jesus told them, 'The rulers of the Gentiles lord it over them . . . Not so with you' (Matthew 20:25–26). In Christian leadership we go down in servanthood rather than up in rank or status. Leaders are prepared to do hard and unpleasant things and go to difficult places because they want to hear 'Well done, good and faithful servant' at the end (Matthew 25:21).

I will never forget my very first day as a young leader on a ministry team. All the juniors were washing the dishes for a large conference. The next training session had already begun when our big boss came in, bringing all his senior team with him. 'We will wash up for you because it's more important that you attend the meeting and get to know the Lord better,' he said. Leaders deliberately put themselves out for the sake of Jesus in other people's lives.

Spiritual leadership isn't first and foremost about activities, position or status. It is about servanthood. Jesus himself said, 'The Son of Man did not come to be served, but to serve, and to give his life as a ransom for many' (Mark 10:45). But this servanthood is not a vaguely defined call to be a doormat. Rather, it is servanthood with a purpose. Spiritual leaders help others know the overflowing love and grace of God, because they are learning to love and know him better and better themselves. Their job is to produce radically God-centred Christians and churches, discipling and equipping others so that they will be concerned for the growth of God's kingdom, and participate in making him famous. Spiritual leaders are leaders of a different kind.

So what should spiritual leaders look like?

- They have a close walk with God. Why would we follow anyone unless that person has a heart that is hot for Jesus? We want to know that they are passionate about God's glory and that they find his Word a daily delight and joy.
- They have a deep desire for their character to be like Jesus. Leaders who are arrogant or power-hungry are not true spiritual leaders. By contrast, spiritual leaders have humble and loving spirits. They are full of thanksgiving and adoration. They put aside their own

interests in order to see Jesus formed in other people's lives. Perhaps most of all they are deeply conscious of God's grace overflowing to them in sin-covering, life-transforming power.
- They have ideas and vision for building up the church, a passion for seeing God's glory spread. They will want the local church to be totally God-centred.

When we see people like this, it is irrelevant whether or not they are formally *called* a leader in their particular church. Biblically, they *are* a leader.

Working for others' progress and joy in God

A leader recently told me, 'I never realized before that the Bible says that my job is to work with people for their joy in God. That's wonderful, and it revolutionizes what I think I should do.' When I ask people what they think they are meant to do as leaders, the most common answers are: look after people's needs and teach the Bible and visit the sick. But, as we've seen, the very heart is working with people for their progress and joy in God.

But this isn't a short-term, quick-fix option. Helping people learn to receive and enjoy God's grace isn't something to be accomplished in brief Sunday meetings alone. Building communities of grace and depth isn't done without a significant commitment of time, vulnerability, trust and accountability.

This is why many churches simply don't do it, but instead choose to interpret leading as the ability to run good meetings, which are so much easier to assess. For years as a young leader, when my boss would ask me, 'What have you done this week?' I found it easier to reply that I had led five Bible studies than to talk about meeting and encouraging a single individual in

God, even though in many cases meeting with ones and twos was much more fruitful. Working for others' progress and joy is not easily evaluated by measurable activity, and yet many churches continue to assess leadership effectiveness this way.

So how do we lead for progress in the faith and joy in God in practice? Here are a few of my top suggestions. It will usually involve:

1. Helping people delight themselves in the Lord. Encouraging them to love God, love the Son of God and love the Holy Spirit. It will include helping them give expression to that love in praise, prayer and adoration.
2. Helping people enjoy God's Word. Leaders often stop a little short by helping people *understand* the Bible, but don't take the next step to helping them use it to *apply, enjoy, obey and worship God*. Understanding is an essential first step in the process, but it isn't the intended final goal.
3. Helping people to be amazed by the benefits of Christ: adoption into God's family, forgiveness from sins and a home in heaven. A heavenly Father who gives freedom from guilt and the curse of the Law. A new heart, new desires, the gift of the Holy Spirit and a great High Priest through whom we have redemption.
4. Helping people grasp the glory of God in the good news of his grace. It says in Romans 5 that we 'reign in life' by receiving God's grace and the gift of eternal life (verse 17). Working with people for their joy will involve helping them to know how to receive God's grace, and seeking God with them for it.
5. Loving people deeply and doing them good, especially if they are in difficulty or distress.

6. Challenging people to take new steps in trusting God and being ambitious about where God might take them in their spiritual walk. Leaders model through their own lives some of what is possible with God.
7. Helping people to pray, showing them how to do it and telling them what we are praying for them.

Spiritual leadership is deeper than any other kind of leadership because it involves developing people's hearts and walk with God, rather than merely running programmes or developing skills. Spiritual leadership is different from worldly leadership because it is concerned more with *spiritual formation* and *life-transformation* than with people merely receiving *information*.

The spiritual production line: Kathy's mistake

Kathy was an apprentice leader who discipled students in her church. She was keen that I should know just how conscientious and hardworking she was. When I asked her how she went about helping others, she said, 'I spend precisely an hour reading the Bible with six students every day of the week.'

'How does that work?' I asked, intrigued.

'I read up on a passage of the Bible, prepare some good questions and interesting thoughts, and then the students come one after another to do my Bible study,' she said. 'That way I can guarantee that the maximum number are getting to know about God through me using my time as efficiently as possible.'

'But surely that doesn't allow deep friendships to form very easily?' I asked her.

'We aren't doing it for friendship,' she said. 'That is much less important than them learning lots about God.'

I pressed her: 'Don't you ever get to the end of the hour and someone tells you there is something really troubling them, or a situation they would like prayer for?'

She looked a little confused. 'No, I can honestly say that has never happened in all the time I have been teaching these students.'

> **To consider:**
>
> - Describe Kathy's understanding of how people grow as Christians. What mistaken assumptions about leadership do you detect in her approach?
> - Do you think Kathy's pattern of working is likely to produce long-term spiritual fruit in lives?

It was very clear, through my conversation with Kathy, that she had swapped transferring information about God for working with a person for their joy in God. It is easy to see why leaders might get sucked into such a pattern when they are pressed for time, and it goes without saying that there is almost always too much to do in leadership.

But Kathy's strategy is flawed. I don't doubt her sincere good intentions, but it is impossible to measure growth in character in that way. Helping people enjoy God requires long-term care, attention and a genuine relationship.

People will hunger for knowledge about God and skills for serving him when they are actually enjoying him. The desire for that knowledge and skills is a by-product of a deepening walk with the Holy Spirit. By contrast, it is quite possible to know the facts and have some idea how to behave 'Christianly' but not to delight oneself in the Lord. That is a recipe for a religion of works in which people confuse being a mature believer with knowing a lot of things.

Knowing information without delight or worship is no good. Developing factual knowledge and intellect is not enough. Neither is building seemingly vibrant activities and meetings. These are only good if people are walking deeper and deeper in the ways of the Lord.

Keeping everyone happy? Returning to John's story

Let's return to John's story. It is a very frequent one in leadership and could just as easily have been about a youth leader, home group leader or PCC member, as about a vicar.

The heart of John's problem is that he is unsure of what is required of a spiritual leader. Either he has never been taught this or he has lost perspective amid the onslaught of competing demands and opinions. In such circumstances it is common for leaders to feel the pressure to do what everyone else wants them to do. Without a core understanding of spiritual leadership in place, John feels obliged to accede to every demand made of him in order to justify his existence. Even if he doesn't know quite what he is meant to be doing, it seems that a lot of other people have clear views on the subject – and will judge him accordingly.

John's definition of success could easily become: 'Have I kept all the plates spinning today?' or 'Have I done enough visible activity to justify my job in the minds of those I serve?' He is being pummelled into doing things he isn't gifted at, at the expense of what he ought to be doing. The Catch 22 is that, if he stops doing some of the things that are expected, the congregation are likely to complain that their favourite activities are being neglected. Many full-time church leaders have told me that they thought they were being invited to lead in mission and discipleship, only to discover after they were appointed that they were actually expected to run themselves ragged serving up everyone's favourite activities.

A final pressure is that John is expected to be a perfectly sinless role model. This has the effect of separating him from the community he leads and turning him into a professional who delivers services that others consume. There is no better way to encourage leaders to wear masks or distance themselves from the church than by making their position dependent on them (or their family) being sinless. A pastor recently said to me, 'I am the only person in the church whose job depends on fooling everyone that I never sin. Other people can talk to me about their sin, but I can't talk to anyone else.'

Getting out of the rut

So what does John need to help him to get out of the rut he's in? The first thing is encouragement from other Christians, with whom he can be himself. Let's face it, he has taken significant steps down the road which will lead to him stalling spiritually. Without such friendships, he is likely to replace his spiritual life with a shallow veneer of godliness and visible activities. Dangerous!

Next, he needs people who share a vision for spiritual leadership that doesn't boil down to simply doing everything that everyone expects of him. Sooner or later he will have to stop doing some things. He will need others to stand with him as he hears people's disappointment and disapproval.

But most of all, John needs people who will feed and encourage him spiritually. He is responsible for taking care of others, but nobody is taking care of him. Ideally, he will find others in the church with whom to share the burdens, but failing that, it is crucial for him to find them outside.

To consider:
If you are a leader, how are you doing? Test your heart:

- Towards God. How would you describe your prayer and worship life? Is your heart happy in God? If not, what are the hindrances you need to address?
- Towards yourself. Would your friends say you are a person of integrity, soft-hearted, humble and discerning?
- Towards others. Would your congregation identify that you are full of love, forgiveness, repentance, kindness and servant-heartedness, with an ability to teach and a desire to see others grow in Jesus?

If you aren't a leader:

- Does your church devote time and manpower to discipling people? Would you say that your leaders understand that their job is to work with believers for their progress and joy in God? If not, why not?
- Do you know who feeds spiritually the leaders who feed you? Or do you just assume it must be happening? (It may well not be.) In what ways might your church further encourage and provide for leaders' spiritual growth as they serve for Jesus' sake?

SECTION 2:
How to grow vibrant leaders in your church

3. CLEAR, DIG AND NURTURE

Main principle: New leaders emerge when there is fertile soil in which they can grow

---

God wants your church to have godly and competent spiritual leaders whose aim is that everyone in the fellowship might grow in their joy in God.

The apostle Paul tells Timothy to put 'identifying leaders' right at the top of his list of priorities: 'The things you have heard me say in the presence of many witnesses entrust to reliable men who will also be qualified to teach others' (2 Timothy 2:2). That's a line of four generations of reliable leaders and teachers, all passing on the baton to the next generation: Paul, Timothy, reliable people and others after them. Teaching new people to lead was top priority for Paul, for he knew that multiplying and teaching new leaders was critical if the churches were to have a flourishing culture of leadership after he was gone.

But how? It's one thing to know that we would like to grow and encourage spiritual leaders, or to take new steps ourselves, but that doesn't necessarily mean that we know how to set about it. What can we actually *do* to begin to turn the dream into reality in our churches?

Divide and plant: Sarah's story

A pastor once invited me to give some training sessions for home group leaders. 'We have one house group that is making an enormous impact,' he told me, 'but we really aren't sure why it is so much more effective than the others.'

'What makes it so remarkable?' I asked.

'It keeps planting new groups. And lots of people really want to be part of it. We don't know any more than that. We have never actually asked the leader. Why don't we ask her during the training?'

So we did. Sarah came to the front, slightly nervously. 'I don't really think we've done anything special,' she said. 'But when I was asked to be a home group leader, I prayed to God for two things. First, that it would be a brilliant group that lots of people would want to be a part of, and secondly that we might divide it and plant another group every year.'

'So how have you acted on that prayer?' we asked.

'I realized that if God was going to make it a brilliant group, then it would be easy to say to everyone in church that it was a wonderful thing to be a part of, and we would love to have them there. So I approached everyone I knew who wasn't already in a group and invited them.' She paused, and then asked the pastor nervously, 'That was all right, wasn't it?'

'Then I realized,' she went on, 'that if we were going to plant a new group every year, I would have to take a new person under my wing and teach them how to lead a group so that they would be ready when the time came. That's really all I've been doing for eight years.'

> **To consider:**
>
> - Why do you think Sarah's strategy was so effective?

As we've seen, Sarah doesn't think of herself as a great leader. She is rarely up at the front and is perfectly ordinary when you meet her. But she has seen God produce lots of other groups and lots of other leaders through her. After she spoke, it was as if scales fell from the eyes of all the other home group leaders in the room. You could see them thinking, 'That's simple. Why on earth didn't I think of it?'

Here is what Sarah did:

1. She really believed that God wanted to grow disciples and develop new leaders through home groups.
2. She wanted to lead a group that people really longed to join because, through it, they would grow in God.
3. She prayed to God about her plans.
4. She enthused to everyone she could.
5. She looked for people to share the job of leading with her.
6. She passed on the baton and multiplied the group whenever it got big enough.

That was all. But it was enough to produce a culture where growth was happening all the time. She was doing what Paul told Timothy to do, and it wasn't especially difficult.

Challenging two wrong ideas about leadership

Let's make it more difficult . . .

Compare Sarah's story to a conversation I had several years ago with a pastor over lunch. I mentioned to him that I was interested in finding ways to help people have a first go at leading. I was astonished by his answer: 'I think we should make it as difficult as we possibly can for people to have a go at leading.'

My mouth dropped open! 'Why? Aren't leaders meant to equip and release every Christian to serve God?'

'That's not the way I see it,' he replied. 'How do you know you won't get people who want to lead just out of personal ambition? How will you prevent them from becoming proud? I think that, if they press on when we make it hard for them, this will show that it really is God calling them. When I trained as a full-time pastor, I had to live in poverty to do so. That's how you identify real spiritual leaders.'

Giving him the benefit of the doubt, it is possible that this pastor had grown up in an environment where some people sought to be leaders for all the wrong reasons. However, there is something fundamentally flawed about his idea, which implies that gifts given by God for the benefit of the body of Christ should be hindered rather than released. This pastor effectively believed that very few people should consider whether God might be giving them gifts for leadership. On the contrary, I think that lots should! The chances are that if you are reading this, you should too!

I asked this man, 'Do you really mean, if you know God has his hand on a person's life for leadership, and they do too, that additional hurdles should be put in their way?'

'When you put it like that, I suppose not,' he conceded, but his face gave him away even as he said it.

Leadership is not a biblical idea

Some time ago a woman challenged me: 'I think your teaching is wrong. There simply isn't any teaching about leadership in the New Testament, as you claim there is. It never uses the word "leadership", but teaches instead about the priesthood of all believers. We all follow Jesus' leadership now, so we don't need to follow human leaders any more.'

This sounds like it might be plausible. After all, the New Testament *does* teach the priesthood of all believers. However, even a quick reading of Paul's letters shows this interpretation to be quite mistaken. There are lots of verses that show that leaders and leadership are a biblical gift that God wants to give to our churches.[1] Here are five of them:

- If [a person's gift] is leadership, let him govern diligently (Romans 12:8).
- Now we ask you, brothers, to respect those who work hard among you, who are over you in the Lord and who admonish you. Hold them in the highest regard in love because of their work (1 Thessalonians 5:12-13).
- The elders who direct the affairs of the church well are worthy of double honour, especially those whose work is preaching and teaching (1 Timothy 5:17).
- Remember your leaders, who spoke the word of God to you. Consider the outcome of their way of life and imitate their faith (Hebrews 13:7).
- Obey your leaders and submit to their authority. They keep watch over you as men who must give an account. Obey them so that their work will be a joy, not a burden, for that would be of no advantage to you (Hebrews 13:17).

God at work! Three steps to preparing the ground

So what can we actually do to begin to create fertile soil for vibrant new leaders to grow in? When we plant a garden, we start by thinking about how to clear the ground. I know a lot about gardening – through diligently watching my wife! When she plants up a flower bed, first she clears out the weeds so that the flowers have a flying start, then she digs in compost to create the best soil, and finally she plants out seedlings that have been encouraged to get the best possible start in life indoors (in small pots covering every surface in my study!).

1. Clear the weeds: Really believe that God wants to grow leaders in your church – and get praying!

The first step to growing flourishing leaders is that a church must believe that God actually wants to give them to us. Leaders will never emerge if the church doesn't expect them, or worse, actively doesn't want them. Not trusting that God wants to provide them is like planting tender young seedlings into a border full of dandelions. The weeds suck all the nutrients out of the soil and kill the plants before they ever get to bloom. I have seen many examples of people with potential never realized because their environment was hostile to them flowering.

Some churches have ceased to believe that their church is the main place for growing leaders. They are therefore unwilling to make it a key priority or give significant time and resources to the job. For many, the only way to develop leaders is to send them off to Bible school or theological college and then buy back leadership fully formed. When this becomes the church's only source of leaders, there will always be a scarcity rather than an abundance.

Sometimes people ask me, 'But what do we do if we simply don't have any leaders?' Just like Sarah, the critical thing is to begin to pray regularly that God will raise them up. He is the gift-giving God. Might a scarcity of leaders come down to something as simple as the fact that we don't ask him? After all, James tells us that we don't have because we don't ask God (James 4:2).

When we start to pray like this, what is happening is that we are beginning to exercise faith. We say to God, 'Father, your children need you. There is something we are lacking, and we can't make it happen ourselves. Please will you give us what we need for your kingdom to grow here among us?' God *loves* that! We are saying, 'We are going to bank our hopes on something we can't arrange ourselves. If God doesn't come through for us, we are stuck.' The reason God likes this so much is that it enables him to show how much he loves and cares for his church. When we only ever attempt things that we can accomplish entirely in our own strength, he is often less inclined to bless our activities because the glory for the success goes to us rather than to him. When we start to pray with faith for him to do things that we can't, the success all belongs to him and he gets the glory.

So the first practical step is to put 'developing leaders' at the top of our church's prayer list. This is the spiritual equivalent of getting out a hoe and severing the roots of the weeds. Let's make this a priority in our services and prayer meetings and private prayer times. Let's get praying friends round for an evening, kneel down and ask God to meet our needs in this area.

One word of warning: people who pray with such a vision frequently end up being part of the answer themselves! Just bear in mind that, if God is stirring you up to believe and pray, he is quite likely also to start giving you a desire to be a spiritual leader. Just so that you know . . .

2. Dig in compost: Be clear about what spiritual leaders are for – and start teaching others

There are many reasons why a church might not want spiritual leaders, but one of the main ones is that they have settled for comfort and familiarity, which the presence of new leaders might challenge. It is a depressingly common story for churches to want leaders simply to run already-established favourite activities. When new leaders instead encourage them to explore fresh challenges with God, they dig in their heels.

Just as a field that grows the same crops year on year will eventually run out of nutrients, so churches which are essentially just weekly repetitions of favourite activities will eventually become spiritually barren. Where people have confused enjoyable activities with being a real biblical church, perhaps for many years, every attempt to shift them out of the rut can be perceived as a threat. Where such a culture dominates a local church, there will be a strong movement to keep things just as they are.

If you want to reignite a fire that has nearly gone out, you have to fan oxygen on to the flames. Those final embers need a breath of fresh air. And if you want a field to return to life, you have to dig in nutrients. The two nutrients that reinvigorate stalling churches and tired disciples are:

A. Teaching from the Bible about what a church actually is. Who couldn't be excited about being part of the bride of Christ? How can people remain ambivalent when they hear about God's great plans for the church? How can people not want to get involved when they realize that the local church is, as Bill Hybels often says, God's hope for the world?
B. Teaching about what spiritual leaders provide – that they are workers for everyone's joy in God.

When these two foundations are laid, everything is in place for a dynamic change of mindset. Seedlings grow best when their roots find this rich soil, rather than struggling hard for every last piece of nourishment.

A different DNA: Adrian's story

I met Adrian at a church leaders' conference in 2006. His church was experiencing rapid growth, lots of new people were becoming Christians, and quite a few were exploring leadership for the first time. I was excited as he spoke about the vision in his church, and everyone else in the room was taking copious notes.

'We want everyone in our church to have a different DNA,' he said. When asked what he meant, he replied, 'In many churches if you ask people why they are there, they can't give you a clear answer. Or they will talk about their favourite activities or groups of friends. We want things to be very different.

'Here we want everyone to be wholly committed to impacting our area with the good news of God's grace in Jesus Christ. We don't want people to join our church for any other reason, but only if they can connect with this vision.'

'Do you think that this focus is responsible for the growth you have experienced?' we asked.

'Yes,' Adrian replied. 'The strange thing is that the growth is at least partly due to the fact that we have made it quite difficult to join the church. People want to be part of a community in which they will be further on with God in a year's time than they are now. Our clear focus provides that confidence.'

Adrian went on to explain that there are two main views of what a local church is, and therefore of what leadership is for. Many churches have what can be described as a 'pastoral' understanding of themselves. They see the job of leaders as catering for the pastoral needs of insiders. The alternative, he suggested, is to understand a local church as a 'prophetic' or 'missional' community, a group for impacting the world with the gospel, with leaders who equip everyone for doing so.

> **To consider:**
>
> - Which view best describes your church? Inward looking (pastoral) or outward facing (missional)? Why?

Our vision for spiritual leadership will largely be shaped by our vision of what a local church is for. If our vision is primarily of a pastoral community, then the kind of leader that will be valued will be a pastoral carer with sensitivity and empathy. If the vision is primarily of a missional community, then the church will be more likely to value and develop leaders who equip everyone to reach outside the walls of the church building.

Without wanting in any way to dismiss the value of good pastoring, the church with a passion for reaching the lost and impacting the world with the good news is much more likely to develop leaders. Their vision is for future change and growth rather than remaining where they are. They are likely to be less concerned about the 'messiness' that comes when less experienced leaders get things wrong. The missional community has a clear idea of where it would like to be several years from now. It will be prayerfully planning for change, and that in itself makes it cry out for God to give leaders. When people are seized with a vision that they want to achieve, the obvious question is: 'What do we need God to provide for us to get going?'

So the second practical step for preparing the ground is to soak ourselves in what the Bible says about the church and leadership.² Rejoice that your local church is a spiritual house where God lives by his Holy Spirit. Love the picture of a church being like a mature man: a vibrant picture of strength and beauty, wisdom and ability. Enjoy being the bride, the body, God's family, a royal priesthood and holy nation. Ask your church leaders for teaching on some of the main passages that explain the nature of the church and the value of spiritual leaders.

3. Nurture seedlings: Encourage people to have a go – and start talent-spotting!

Almost all churches choose leaders to meet a current urgent need. This isn't always a bad thing. In Acts 6 a need arose to make sure that food was distributed fairly and wisely, so the apostles looked for people who were full of the Holy Spirit and wisdom, who could step up to the plate (no pun intended!) and take responsibility.

However, if that is the only way we ever approach the task of identifying leaders, then we will always find ourselves plugging gaps as they become apparent. We won't train leaders according to our future vision, but simply in order to keep things running as they have always run: 'We have a crisis in the old folks group and need another hand on deck. Right, you'll do!'

It is an essential foundation of good leadership to develop leaders for the growth you wish to support *before* you need them to assume responsibility. Any good gardener starts seeds off in a gentle, kind environment, like a greenhouse. They don't throw new plants straight into an inhospitable place that will be too challenging for their survival.

Most people in your church will assume that the early nurture of leaders is the sole responsibility of the main church leader, and it will of course be one of their most important jobs. But remember Sarah. She decided as a young home group leader that she could encourage others to have a go at leading with her. Not only was this critical subsequently for multiplying groups, but she could actually do it in a way that her church leader couldn't. It was much less scary, for example, for Sarah to say, 'Would you like to lead an evening Bible study with me?' than if the pastor did so! Sarah provided the greenhouse. Being with her was a safe and sheltered place out of the public gaze.

You don't have to be a highly visible, full-time leader to be able to look out for people whom the Lord might be encouraging to have a go. In fact, if it is only left to the full-time leader, then lots of potential talent will fall between the cracks. The best scouts for future spiritual leaders in your church might well be ordinary people just like you.

Get ahead of the game: David's story

Over a cup of coffee I asked David, a church leader, how new leaders are trained in his church.

'The issue you ought to think about isn't "how we do it" but "when",' he replied. 'We always train more leaders than we actually need at any given time.'

'But isn't that a waste of energy?' I asked.

'Absolutely not,' he said. 'Not only is investment in their skills and character useful in its own right – even if they never lead a group – but it means that we always have a ready supply of leaders if, for example, we want to start a new home group.'

'What are the main, positive consequences for your church?' I asked. He could list three straightaway.

'First, we never have to put our vision on hold while we identify leaders. Secondly, we never have a situation where a small number of leaders feel they are carrying far too many responsibilities. And thirdly, it is quite normal for people to try leading for the first time. Our home group leaders are always looking out for possible new leaders, even if they are only very tentative, so everyone gets used to it. And we all expect that we will have vibrant leadership across all aspects of church life. This has become normal. And all these benefits come from placing a high value on letting people try things out.'

The third practical step to growing flourishing leaders is therefore to encourage people to have a go in a safe and gentle environment. Ease them in, allowing enough time in the greenhouse before they are transplanted to the harsh outdoors. Nobody ever finds out what they are gifted or ungifted at until they have a chance to try. The church that only ever lets a few people – or one person – have a go, for fear of failure, will not release the spiritual gifts of everyone who comes. It is really important to model that failure *is* an option. Of course we don't want to enshrine failure and doing things badly, but if we only value success, many people will never try anything for fear of not doing well enough.

It's OK to find out: Philip's story

Philip is a friend of mine at church. He loves the Bible and is good with words, so we encouraged him to try giving a sermon. To start with, he was nervous, understandably, but we assured him that it was safe, helped him prepare, and encouraged him with feedback afterwards.

After several attempts, however, it was clear that he simply wasn't comfortable. 'I don't think this particular leadership role is the one God wants for me,' he confessed.

And that was fine. He had had a go and had found out something that he wouldn't otherwise have known. He was encouraged that others thought that God might be giving him some gifts to use in church and he had honed some skills along the way. He subsequently led a flourishing home group, helping people apply God's Word to their lives, and loved it.

Does your church want to grow?

You can be one of God's talent scouts! You might even be able to see what God is doing in someone's life when others have missed it. You might be able to see potential for serving God that the person himself can't see. Looking for future leaders doesn't require you to have a PhD in theology, just to want to encourage others to discover and use the gifts God is giving them to build up the church.

Let's return to where we started in this chapter. Do you want your church to have spiritual leaders? If most people have no personal commitment to extending God's kingdom, then it is very hard – perhaps impossible – to persuade them of the need. Without an expectation that God wants to build the church, there is no reason to desire that he should give leaders.

If, on the other hand, your church is excited about growth and really wants to see God work, then persuading the church of the value of developing leaders is much easier, even if you are few in number. The ground is getting broken up, ready to receive the seedlings. Seeds grow where the environment is conducive. *You* can play a vital part as one of God's gardeners. It might take a while to see the results – after all, flowers don't reveal their full glory until they are fully grown. But don't lose heart. God loves to have you working with him to prepare his garden, and he is not stingy with his blessings.

To consider:

- How can your church prioritize prayer for God to grow leaders?
- Do you know anyone whom you could encourage to try to take some first steps in leading, perhaps heading a small Bible discussion initially or praying aloud in church?
- Ask God to give you a vision like Sarah to pray and enthuse others about God building his church.

4. DEVELOPING YOURSELF AS A SPIRITUAL LEADER

Main principle: Growing spiritual leaders always make time to nurture their hunger for God and their service of other people

---

As we have seen, the heart of being a spiritual leader is serving other people so that they can progress in their faith and know for themselves abundant joy in Jesus Christ. The life of every Christian should be dedicated to the amazing good news of God's grace being received and enjoyed by all people, everywhere. Anyone who deliberately helps other Christians towards this goal is exercising spiritual leadership to some degree, participating in shaping God's community into what it should be and do. The number of spiritual leaders therefore is far greater than just those who lead from up front (although we hope that they will have spiritual leadership gifts too!).

Because of this, it is crucial that leaders have a close walk with God. There is an unbreakable link between the quality of a person's leadership and their relationship with God. Leaders who aren't delighting themselves in the Lord, aren't enjoying the church and are finding the task a drag aren't being good spiritual leaders, regardless of how much skill they might have.

Growing and teachable? Ben and Jane

Ben was twenty-two and, by his own admission, pretty clueless. He had been a Christian a year when I met him on an overseas trip.

'I became a Christian while away from home,' he told me. 'As soon as it happened, I had a sense God wanted me here in this country. So I bought a plane ticket and came over!'

'What, just like that?' I asked.

'Pretty much. Boy, I'm not sure I would do it the same way again, but I love church life here and am getting to know all the non-Christian friends of the youth group. In fact, last night we had a sleepover in the bush and spent all night telling a hundred of them about Jesus. Some have become Christians.

'My difficulty,' he continued, 'is that I don't really know what I'm doing. I try to lead Bible studies, but I don't think I'm very good at it. I wonder if God wants me to be a leader, but I don't know who to ask to help me. I really mucked up last week when someone asked me for advice about a relationship. In fact, I often don't know whether I'm doing the right things or the wrong ones. I'm really jealous of Timothy in the Bible. Paul looked after him and taught him everything. How do I find someone to do that for me?'

Jane was very active in her church. She led a house group, chaired the finance board, gave out the hymn books and arranged the flowers.

When the pastor announced that he intended to get the house group leaders together to pray and think about how they might develop as leaders in the coming year, Jane's response was a polite 'no, thank you'.

'I am genuinely too busy to carve out the additional time,' she said. 'You know I'm committed to something every night of the week. I simply feel that one more straw would break the camel's back.'

'Come on, Jane,' the pastor coaxed. 'Some of the young people would like to begin to learn to lead Bible studies. Why not join us?'

'I already know how to lead Bible studies. I've been doing it for half my life. My group are very happy with what I do and wouldn't want it to change.'

'We are also going to be thinking about how the house groups can deepen their friendships and prayer for one another,' the pastor said.

'But my group know one another very well already. And I devote a lot of time to preparing deep Bible studies. My group really want to be together and they know their Bibles better than anyone else in the church. That's the definition of a flourishing house group.'

The pastor finally caved in. Jane's group did have a very strong group identity and good Bible knowledge. Maybe that was all he should ask of someone who carried so many responsibilities already.

To consider:

- There are genuine advantages to being in the groups led by both Ben and Jane. Which would you rather be a part of and why?

Competent or growing?

Ben isn't very good at what he does, but he is teachable and keen to grow. Jane is evidently good at what she does and devotes a lot of time to making sure it is top-notch. She has a lot more knowledge and skills than Ben, but Ben is keen to develop and is aware of his weaknesses.

I've met Ben and Jane and I like them both. If I had to make a choice about which group I would rather be part of, however, personally I would choose Ben's because he clearly wants to grow spiritually. He wants God to take him on a journey. It is less clear that Jane does. And maybe there is a hint that she thinks about leadership more in terms of her undoubted skills than in terms of enjoyment of a deepening relationship with God.

That is not to say that Jane's desire for her group to know the Bible in depth is wrong – quite the opposite in fact: it is essential. However, the goal of leadership is not, finally, that people know all the facts about God, but that they are being transformed. Personal spiritual growth, local church growth, and growth in depth of a godly community are all connected to whether leaders themselves are growing spiritually.

Do you want to grow?

A good spiritual leader isn't the person who has 'arrived' and got it all right, but a person who knows that they need continually to grow with God and learn from mistakes. I love it when the Gospels record how often the disciples misunderstood and made mistakes. Even after three years with Jesus, when they arrived at the Last Supper, they still weren't one hundred per cent sure who Jesus was! That makes me feel a lot better when I am stupid and slow to get it. One of the best leaders I know likens what he adds to God's work to what a brand new apprentice adds to a carpet-fitter's work – nothing at all! The real reason for the carpet-fitter to have an apprentice isn't that the apprentice makes a brilliant contribution, but so that they will learn to be like the carpet-fitter.

I find it strange that, when many churches think about leaders, they automatically assume that means a fully formed high degree of gifting, usually backed up with a university level education. Would your church ever allow a completely uneducated fisherman from Galilee to be the main leader? If the answer is 'no', then this could be a sign that you are looking for the wrong things.

I haven't arrived. As I look back over the graph of my own spiritual growth, I wish it were a continuous, unbroken upward slope, but it isn't – and neither is anyone else's. It is punctuated with slips and slides, plateaux and potholes, just like yours. A friend at our church recently said to me, 'I always thought leaders were on an exalted plane, inaccessible to the rest of us. But now I realize that you are just as prone to mistakes and temptation as I am. If God can use you, then he can probably use anyone – including me.' I often feel as though people learn more from seeing my mistakes and doing their best not to replicate them than from the things I do well! I thank God every day that he doesn't kick us out of leadership every time we get things wrong. I would have gone a long time ago if that had been the case.

When Paul wanted to help Timothy to grow as a leader, he gave him some crucial advice: 'Watch your life and doctrine closely. Persevere in them, because if you do, you will save both yourself and your hearers' (1 Timothy 4:16). And, interestingly, Timothy was meant to let 'everyone . . . see [his] progress' (verse 15). Sometimes leaders seem to think that being a role model means looking faultless. Not so for Paul and Timothy. They wanted to be transparent about how they were learning and growing, so that other people could learn by watching them.

So what practical steps can we take?

What can we actually do to develop as spiritual leaders? You might not be very far along the road yet, but that doesn't matter. The important thing is not where you are right now, but the direction in which you're travelling. Where would you like to be with God as a leader in a year's time? How can you as a leader watch your life and doctrine closely? Sometimes I rephrase it like this:

- 'Watch your life' means developing a hunger for God and a desire to be like Jesus in your character.
- 'Watch your doctrine' means developing a hunger for God's Word and a love for the people you lead in following it.

Develop a hunger for God

The Psalms are full of emotion about God. The psalmists constantly tell us how to desire him. The greatest possible joy is to be with God and know him deeply and closely:

> How lovely is your dwelling-place,
>   O Lord Almighty!
> My soul yearns, even faints,
>   for the courts of the Lord;
> my heart and my flesh cry out
>   for the living God.
> (Psalm 84:1–2)

O God, you are my God,
> earnestly I seek you;
my soul thirsts for you,
> my body longs for you,
in a dry and weary land
> where there is no water.
(Psalm 63:1)

You can hear the delight and yearning:

As the deer pants for streams of water,
> so my soul pants for you, O God.
(Psalm 42:1)

The single most important foundation for developing ourselves as leaders is learning to desire God like this. The most spiritually crippling thing in the life of a leader is to neglect it. Given that the foundational task of spiritual leaders is to help others make progress and have joy in God, it stands to reason that this is also true for them, maybe even more so.

Whenever I meet a Christian leader, the first thing I want to know about them is whether or not they are falling more and more in love with Jesus. Are they encountering God and enjoying spending time in his presence? Are they enjoying his Word and finding it a source of wonder and worship? When I find people who are transparently adoring, pursuing and worshipping Jesus with all their hearts, I want to spend time with them and learn to be like them.

Ask God for grace

How do we learn to deepen our hunger for God? Can this, in fact, be learned? I believe it can. Paul tells the Romans that we 'reign in life' by receiving 'God's abundant provision of grace and of the gift of righteousness' (Romans 5:17). We reign – that is, we live with God and become more like Jesus – by actively receiving his grace. And the way to do this is very simple: ask God. Pray to him to reveal more and more of the wonder of his grace in Jesus to you every day. When we get a taste of how amazing he is, then we begin to yearn for and desire more and more of God, just like the psalmists did.

I recently asked our home group for practical ideas about how to remember to ask God for grace. Here were some of their answers:

- Write down some of the blessings of knowing God and stick them on your fridge.
- Remind ourselves about God's grace (i.e. that he considers us completely right with himself because of Jesus) every time the church meets, and put it in the weekly bulletin.
- Make friends whom you can call on to ask for prayer that God would give you more and more of himself every day.
- Write down things you don't understand about God's grace so that you can ask your home group leader about them. (The home group leader wasn't so keen on this one!)
- Replace all the church business meetings with meetings about how to grow in grace (my favourite idea, but the pastor didn't like it much!).

These are all great answers, and just as applicable to leaders as to every Christian. The group wanted to talk about grace, rejoice in God's grace together, tell one another what God was doing in their lives and spur one another on to seek God more and more.

How is your worship life going?

Grace flows to hearts that are open to receive it. King David was a man after God's heart. The one thing he wanted most in his life wasn't to be a great king or a wonderful leader, but this:

> . . . that I may dwell in the house of the Lord
>   all the days of my life,
> to gaze upon the beauty of the Lord
>   and to seek him in his temple.
> (Psalm 27:4)

This is the reason why he was a great leader. His deepest desire was simply to gaze. He wanted to saturate himself with the beauty of God and seek him. These two things always go together. If you love someone, you enjoy being with them. You want to belong to them.

So it is always helpful to know how a leader's prayer and worship life are going. Are they full of thankfulness to God? Are they finding it easy to express their adoration to him? Are there any factors in their life that are hindering their prayers and killing their worship? Where such factors exist, it doesn't necessarily mean that this person shouldn't be a leader, but it is a clear indication that something needs to change in order for them to continue to grow.

The nitty-gritty

So let's get down to the real nitty-gritty. I said that it is possible to learn to hunger for God. In appendix 1 you will find some questions to help you consider how your walk with God is going. I want you to pause at this point and take a good look at these questions. Try to be honest with yourself. You don't have to show your answers to anyone, but you might find it helpful to do so.

* * *

I hope you didn't find the questions too intimidating. The point isn't to load you with guilt if you are doing badly, or make you think, 'Where am I going to find the time to fix all this?' The point is to clarify your focus on spiritual growth and provide some possible starting points for taking a next step with God. It is one thing knowing that we would *like* to grow, but actually *growing* requires us to get deliberate and practical.

Hungering for God's Word

Here's one simple but devastating truth: if we neglect God's Word, the Bible, then we wither and die as spiritual leaders.

Paul says that the Word teaches, corrects, rebukes and trains us in righteousness so that we can be thoroughly equipped. Treating it negligently is a fast route to plateauing out. Jesus told the disciples, 'Remain in me, and I will remain in you . . . you [cannot] bear fruit unless you remain in me' (John 15:4). How do we remain in Jesus and not lose our spiritual fruitfulness? Jesus continued: 'If you remain in me and *my words remain in you*, ask whatever you wish, and it will be given you' (verse 7, my emphasis).

And yet I have met leaders, both young and old, who are tempted to snack on the Bible rather than savour it. One reason stands out above all others for this neglect: busyness. We live such fast, crazily packed-out lives that we find it incredibly difficult to free up the time to drink deeply from the Bible, and when we do so, we can feel guilty that we aren't rushing off to do something else.

The way this danger surfaces for me as a preacher is that I read the Bible in order to teach it rather than because I am thirsting to know God. This means that my leadership ceases to flow *from* my walk with God and instead *replaces it*. That is no longer valuable spiritual leadership. Satan uses busyness to destroy effective leadership. It is the chief weapon in his armoury to blunt my spiritual cutting edge. And I can easily collude in the process by not stopping to ask how I am doing, just in case I don't like the answers.

A number of years ago, I was walking through London with two well-known church leaders, both a generation older than me. Keen to learn from them, I asked, 'Tell me, how are your devotions going and what is God doing in your lives?' One of them replied, 'I can't remember the last time anyone asked me a question like that.' The other burst into tears and told me that his life had felt spiritually dry for more years than he cared to remember. Whenever you meet a mature Christian leader, you should ask them if their private devotions are keeping their walk with the Lord energized.

How to disciple others for their progress and joy

Having considered how we grow as leaders, let's now see how we grow in *leadership*.

Once again I would like you to get really practical by turning to the second review exercise in appendix 2 which is all about serving other people, in order that they make progress in their faith and have joy in God. Turn back to this page when you have had the chance to reflect.

* * *

How did you get on? Maybe it felt a little strange to be precise and focused about areas in which we seek to grow as spiritual leaders. But much growth simply doesn't happen because we don't deliberately plan to grow. Unless we are intentional, we won't organize our time or activities to help serve our growth as leaders. We won't set any goals or have a strategy for taking the next steps. I regularly meet people just like Jane in the story at the start of the chapter. They may be competent, but feel no incentive to go any further. Leaders can stagnate, even if it seems to everyone else that they are delivering what is expected of them.

Three practical steps

So how can we plan to grow as leaders over the long haul? I try to ensure that I have the following three practical helps in my life. I think they are valuable in the life of any leader:

1. Find a mentor

I am continually tempted to live an unexamined life. Maybe you are too. It's not that we don't want people to get close to us, it's just that we don't want to carve out the necessary time. But this means that I can run from pillar to post, never stopping long enough to receive care for my soul or leadership from others.

There is an unbreakable link between flourishing in spiritual leadership and the spiritual care and counsel we receive. I am suspicious of those who lead in splendid isolation and never let anyone get close enough to see their struggles. I am really glad that I have friends who won't let me get away with that. They *insist* on caring for me, rebuking me where necessary and holding me to account, because they want me to enjoy a close walk with God.

> **To consider:**
> Do you have people whom you can talk to in depth about:
>
> - How you would like to grow as a Christian and as a leader in the coming year?
> - The joys and struggles in your spiritual life?
> - Your attitudes and sin patterns?

If you are reluctant to share these kinds of things with reliable friends or be accountable to them, what do you think is at the root of this? Receiving encouragement is vital to our joy in the Lord. When we have appropriate support, it is so much easier to grow. Without it, it is much harder to know whether or not we are growing or doing the right things as leaders.

The older we get, the fewer the people who are likely to participate with us in our growth. Those we have looked to in the past may move away or even die. Younger people find it hard to encourage older leaders. When I had been a leader in a mission organization for a number of years, a humble, prayerful man in his late teens said to me, 'I may be wrong, but I think you're struggling in a particular area and need some encouragement. And I think I should be that encourager.' He was over a decade younger than me but he had hit the nail on the head. It was a real risk for him to ask if he could help me, but he did a great job and is still a close friend to this day (and, no surprise here, an excellent pastor in his church!).

Look out for older believers whom you can ask to teach and lead you. Look for peers with whom to build spiritual friendships with openness, honesty and mutual encouragement. I meet three times a year with a group of leaders of my own age so we can pray and encourage one another with complete frankness and honesty. But don't forget also that younger people can still be mature Christians. Paul told Timothy to teach the older men. The older we get, the greater the percentage of godly spiritual leaders who will be younger than us. We need humility to realize that God may want to use them to feed us.

2. Start making deliberate plans

As you have read this chapter, you have worked through review exercises, one about your spiritual walk and the other about your growth as a spiritual leader. Now it is time to turn your reflections into a plan.

Look back at the notes you made. From each exercise, write down the top two areas in which you want to grow over the next six months or year. Why have you chosen these priorities?

Next, decide how you will seek to grow in the areas you have identified. Will it be through asking someone to teach or guide you? Through taking part in some activity in which you will learn by experience? Through reading or attending a training course? Through establishing spiritual accountability with another person for an aspect of your spiritual walk? As you answer the question: 'How am I going to do this?', it will be very helpful if you write down the goals you would like to have achieved by three months, six months, nine months and a year.

Finally, discuss your plan with another leader whom you trust. Let him or her help you shape or alter it if necessary, making suggestions about how to arrange your time and priorities in order to achieve your goal. Then make a diary note six months from now to review with them how you are doing.

3. Saturate yourself with leadership wisdom

For me, the most important question about how to grow as a leader is: 'Where can I find wise advice?' I will never figure out how to do everything on my own, so it's crucial to get wisdom from outside sources.

Of course the first place to go is to the Bible. It has so much to say about spiritual leadership. And I want to know everything it says! I want wisdom from God pumping through my veins. It is vital that I know what Paul tells Timothy about the character that is necessary for leaders. And how can I be ignorant of what Titus is told that leaders should teach others? It would be crazy not to read up on biblical examples of bad leaders, in order to make sure I don't make the same mistakes, and similarly crazy not to discover everything I can about the most godly leaders in the Bible so that they can be my role models. I want to hear Jesus telling his disciples the purpose of the church, so that I know what leaders ought to do. Saturate yourself with leadership lessons from Scripture!

But while the Bible is the main source of leadership wisdom, it isn't the only one. I also want to find out everything I can from other leaders. The way the first disciples learned was by being with Jesus, watching him, and then being sent out to have a go themselves. They were apprentices. I want other leaders to let me be an apprentice too. I want to know about their struggles and how they receive resources to overcome them. I want to know how they lead in situations that I don't yet understand. I want to find out how they read the Bible, pray and worship. I love every valuable opportunity to sit down with them and discover how they deal with difficulties and setbacks. I want to attend courses and training events where trustworthy individuals share how God has used them. Basically, I want to download their brains so that I can benefit from their experience. I want them to walk with me as I learn from their example.

As I mentioned, I work for a ministry called Living Leadership which runs a training programme for junior leaders in churches. One of the most important elements is having experienced leaders share about themselves and what they do. They talk about their mistakes as well as their successes, their struggles with sin as well as their triumphs, their devotional practices as well as how they lead. The trainees always say that this is one of the most helpful things in the programme, but sadly they are usually surprised to hear leaders being open about the difficulties and struggles of being a spiritual leader rather than just recounting the good parts.

Finally, I love to receive wisdom from leaders who are no longer alive! The best leaders read everything they can from the best leaders of the past, as well as the present, accessing godly wisdom from across centuries and across the world. Often I prefer dead writers to living ones, but there are many helpful books today as well. (I have listed some great books on leadership in the 'Further reading' section at the end of this book.)

The call to leadership is a call to sacrifice

I hope you are now buzzing with ideas about how you can grow as a leader. But maybe you are also feeling that it seems like a lot of effort. You are wondering how you can find the time.

There are no easy fixes. Spiritual leadership is not a cakewalk. In Acts 20, Paul describes the task of testifying to the gospel of God's grace. He says the job is accompanied by tears, plots from enemies, hard work and lack of personal safety. Spiritual leadership sometimes attracts severe opposition, and it always requires leaders to outdo others in humility – no mean feat. It brings few rewards in worldly terms. It involves compassion, bravery, sacrifice and even, for many leaders down the ages and around the world today, dying. It consumes your whole life.

It's hard, but it's also glorious. Paul says that the gospel of grace is more important than *life itself*. Therefore, being a leader who helps others to know and enjoy the grace of God in Jesus is worth doing at the risk of life, and with the whole of our lives. Leaders have a job that is compellingly wonderful. We help people come to the fountain of life where they receive infinite and astonishing blessing from God. We work as God's undershepherds to help people abandon themselves to him. No wonder the Bible says that leadership is a noble task to be desired (1 Timothy 3:1).

Let's conclude with famous words about spiritual leadership by Howard Guinness. This challenge has gripped me ever since I first read it two decades ago:

> Where are the young men and women of this generation who will hold their lives cheap, and be faithful even unto death? Where are those who will lose their lives for Christ's sake – flinging them away for love of him? Where are those who will live dangerously and be reckless in his service? Where are his *lovers* – those who love him and the souls of men more than their own reputations or comfort, or very life?
>
> Where are the men who say 'no' to self; who take up Christ's cross to bear it after him; who are willing to be nailed to it in college or office, home or mission field; who are willing, if need be, to bleed, to suffer and to die on it?
>
> Where are the men of vision today? Where are the men of enduring vision? Where are the men who have seen the King in his beauty, by whom from henceforth all else is counted but refuse that they may win Christ? Where are the adventurers, the explorers, the pioneers for God who count one human soul of far greater value than the rise or fall of an empire? Where are the men of glory in God-sent loneliness, difficulties, persecutions, misunderstandings, discipline, sacrifice, death?

Where are the men who are willing to pay the price of vision?

Where are the men of prayer? Where are the men who, like the psalmist of old, count God's Word of more importance to them than their daily food? Where are the men who, like Moses, commune with God face to face as a man speaks with his friend, and unmistakably bear with them the fragrance of the meeting through the day?

Where are God's men in this day of God's power?[1]

As I write this last sentence, I am praying that you too will long to be such a person.

To consider:

- Which godly leaders do you most admire? What have you learned from them?
- Who will you ask to invest time in your spiritual life and leadership? What qualities do they have that you most wish to emulate?

5. LEADERS WHO LOVE THE HOLY SPIRIT AND THE BIBLE

Main principle: Spiritual leaders are identified by their desire to live by the Holy Spirit, under the authority of the Bible

---

If you asked a random cross-section of people in your church, 'What do you think spiritual leadership is?', what do you think they would say? The people who stand up at the front to teach? The minister? The worship leader or youth pastor?

Listen to how Paul describes his leadership work in Colossians:

> Now I rejoice in what was suffered for you, and I fill up in my flesh what is still lacking in regard to Christ's afflictions, for the sake of his body, which is the church. I have become its servant by the commission God gave me to present to you the word of God in its fulness – the mystery that has been kept hidden for ages and generations, but is now disclosed to the saints. To

them God has chosen to make known among the Gentiles the glorious riches of this mystery, which is Christ in you, the hope of glory.

We proclaim him, admonishing and teaching everyone with all wisdom, so that we may present everyone perfect in Christ. To this end I labour, struggling with all his energy, which so powerfully works in me.
(Colossians 1:24–29)

The first thing that leaps off the page is the strange statement that Paul wants to fill up in his flesh what is lacking in Christ's afflictions. This doesn't mean that there was anything lacking in Christ's sacrifice for us. He isn't suggesting that Jesus' ministry and atoning death were in some way deficient. He means that he, Paul, is working, at the cost of physical hardship, to hold out the blessings of Jesus' suffering, death and resurrection, to everyone. The way he does this is to present the good news in all its fullness. This presentation involves him proclaiming Jesus, admonishing and teaching about him with all wisdom, in order that everyone might know Christ and become mature in him. As he does so, he is deeply aware that it isn't his own energy, but the power of God's Holy Spirit that is at work.

I find two main lessons in this passage which go right to the heart of spiritual leadership:

- Spiritual leaders love and proclaim the message about Jesus so that others can get to know and grow in him.
- They do so, not in their own strength, but in the power of the Holy Spirit.

I seem to be stuck: Dan's story

Dan is a mature Christian. He came to faith ten years ago and has been thoroughly involved in serving God in his church. Over the last year, however, he has started to feel like he is a bit stuck in a rut. He doesn't sense a deepening awareness of God working in his life. He is grateful for every answer to prayer, but he doesn't see a great deal more fruit than he did five years ago, and maybe less than just after he became a Christian. He enjoys serving, and wishes there was a chance to learn new ways to do so, but he doesn't really know how.

Dan asks his minister, 'How can I take new steps with God? I don't want to be in the same place in a year's time.'

'If you want to know more about God,' replies the minister, 'get into the Bible some more. Learn to understand parts of it in greater depth. This will give you a deeper sense of how wonderful God is.'

Dan pauses. That *sounds* like it is a right answer. But he still has some nagging questions, ones that he is a bit embarrassed to ask in case it sounds as if he isn't interested in the Bible. Bravely he presses on.

'I really love the Word, pastor, but I'm not sure that that's the heart of my problem. I don't just want to know it better, I want to find out how I can better live it out and do what it says. When I read about what God did in the early church, it often seems like a far cry from my own experience. How can I see God working more? How can I work with him? How can I grow in serving him? Most people just tell me to read the Bible and pray more if I want to know about God, but I don't just want to know more about him. I want to *know* him. Is there anything, practically, that I can do?'

> **To consider:**
>
> - Have you ever felt stuck in a rut, like Dan?
> - What helped you escape from it (if you feel you have escaped)?
> - Why is 'read the Bible and pray more' (a *correct* answer) sometimes not a *satisfying* answer when we want to know how to grow in God?

Let's take the two main lessons from Colossians in reverse order.

How can I live by the Holy Spirit?

Pause for a moment and jot down your thoughts on this question: what does the Bible mean when it talks about 'living by the Holy Spirit'?

This question takes us right to the heart of spiritual living and serving. Leadership is a gift from the Holy Spirit. Therefore we need to consider what it means, in practice, for leaders (and all Christians) to live by, and be led by, the Spirit of God.

The New Testament uses the phrase in several places, often to contrast living as a Christian with the old life before we came to Christ. For example:

- The righteous requirements of [God's Law are] fully met in us, who do not live according to the sinful nature but according to the Spirit (Romans 8:4).
- So I say, live by the Spirit, and you will not gratify the desires of the sinful nature (Galatians 5:16).
- If you are led by the Spirit, you are not under law (Galatians 5:18).

But what *is* living by the Spirit? *How* can Dan be *led* by the Spirit? By miraculous signs and prophetic words? I believe in both, but that is not the Bible's definition. One of the clearest passages is Galatians 5:5–6: 'But by faith we eagerly await through the Spirit the righteousness for which we hope. For in Christ Jesus neither circumcision nor uncircumcision has any value. The only thing that counts is faith expressing itself through love.' This tells us that we are waiting for the hope that God has for us when we finally meet Jesus. That wait is full of excited anticipation because the Holy Spirit is producing faith in us. Whenever we think ahead to all the blessings we are going to receive and feel our hearts leap, that is the Holy Spirit at work, making us eager.

Notice what the Spirit of God pours into us as we wait: faith that expresses itself through love. That is the heart of what the Bible means when it talks about living by the Holy Spirit:

- We live by faith.
- We trust the Lord for the things we haven't yet received and eagerly look forward to them.
- We work out our faith in love to others.

That is the life the Holy Spirit wants to lead us into, a life full of receiving the love of Jesus and passing it on to others; a life full of the hope of heaven.

How to do it: Being practical

I hope you are asking yourself the question: 'How can I grow? Practically speaking, what can I do in order to live more and more by the Holy Spirit?' The Bible says that if we want to live by the Spirit, we have to be led by the Spirit.

It was our desires that led us before we became Christians. We let them determine what we bought, where we went and how we thought. I and my desires were at the centre of my life, my decisions and my life-direction.

However, when we became Christians, God gave us *new* desires. We no longer want to pursue our own interests, but his. About these new desires the Bible says:

> So I say, live by the Spirit, and you will not gratify the desires of the sinful nature. For the sinful nature desires what is contrary to the Spirit, and the Spirit what is contrary to the sinful nature. They are in conflict with each other, so that you do not do what you want.
> (Galatians 5:16–18)

> Those who live according to the sinful nature have their minds set on what that nature desires; but those who live in accordance with the Spirit have their minds set on what the Spirit desires. The mind of sinful man is death, but the mind controlled by the Spirit is life and peace.
> (Romans 8:5–6)

Where once we had only one set of desires, now we have two, in competition with each other.

Here are three practical steps for being led by the Holy Spirit rather than living according to the sinful nature (i.e. pretending we are following God while still putting the desire for self at the centre):

1. Ask for God's help to set your mind on the new desires from the Holy Spirit.
2. When you are faced with a choice between which set of desires to follow, deliberately choose those that come

from the Holy Spirit. It is usually quite obvious which is which, but that doesn't always mean it is easy to take the right road. Sin can be very alluring or else we wouldn't be tempted by it. At the point of temptation, we consciously have to remind ourselves again and again of who we have become in Jesus: children of God who have been given his righteousness. Over time, we will develop a tendency to lean towards the Holy Spirit's desires rather than those of the sinful nature.

3. Express your faith in God and your new Spirit-given desires by replacing selfish love for yourself with practical, godly love for other people. Not only is this Spirit-filled living, it also reinforces your new desires through practice.

This is how to be led by the Spirit. It is also how to use spiritual gifts correctly: to serve others in love. Dan's problem is not at step one or two. He really wants to follow. But he has no fresh outlets through which to express his faith and spiritual desire. His minister's answer was to encourage him to learn more about God rather than helping him find further ways of putting his faith into practice. But faith that has no opportunity to be practised and lived out soon stops growing.

Being a Spirit-filled leader

This brings us to the issue of how to be Holy Spirit-led leaders. The chief distinguishing mark will be that they want to grow in knowing God and desiring what the Holy Spirit desires.

It is tempting to want to define Spirit-filled leaders as those who have strong Bible knowledge, prophetic gifts or words of knowledge, all real and wonderful gifts from God to the church which leaders may also have. However, the primary defining mark is that they serve other people in love, so that God receives glory. The connection is made very clearly in 1 Timothy 3:13. Speaking about leaders, Paul says that those who 'have *served* well gain an excellent standing and great assurance' (my emphasis).

Leaders don't grow just by knowing a lot of spiritual things. Non-Christians can know a lot about the Bible, but this doesn't mean that they are living by the Holy Spirit. Indeed *Satan* knows a lot of facts about God, and he definitely isn't!

Pause to pray

You might like to take a few minutes at this point to pray, for yourself and for other leaders in your church, that God will help you:

- To set your desires on what the Holy Spirit desires
- To find fresh ways to serve others in love, so that they will get to know God

I like to pray this often for myself and other leaders I know. I want God to set our desires more and more on what the Spirit desires, because that is true godliness.

How will I know if it's working?

You might be wondering if there is a practical way to know whether or not you are making progress in living by the Spirit. You will be pleased to know that there is. Growing in Spirit-filled servant-heartedness and love is demonstrated (or disproved) by our attitudes and character. We cannot claim that we are serving in love if our attitudes don't bear this out. The contradiction will be plain for everyone else to see, even if we kid ourselves. We can undermine how we *say* we want to walk with God by what we are actually like.

It is worth reading what 1 Timothy 3 says about good leadership, and what 2 Timothy 2:14 – 3:9 says about bad leadership. There we discover that good leadership is almost all about character and attitude. Paul tells Timothy that, if he models godly character and attitude, and leads others to do the same, then he is a good leader (1 Timothy 4:6).

2 Timothy 3, however, shows the opposite. Bad leaders love themselves and money, don't love people, and love worldly pleasure rather than God. The scary thing is that the individuals in question are making out that they are Christian leaders – they have a veneer of godliness but deny its power (3:5).

Make no mistake, we have to be discerning. There will be people in churches who claim to be believers, who may have been around for a long time and style themselves as leaders, but who are nothing of the sort. In Acts 20:29–30 Paul warns that 'savage wolves will come in among you and will not spare the flock. Even from your own number men will arise and distort the truth in order to draw away disciples after them. So be on your guard!'

We need to exercise great care before we conclude that someone is a wolf disguised as a spiritual leader. But the more common danger is that churches never do so, for fear of causing disagreement or hurt, and are spiritually damaged or destroyed as a result. Paul says to have nothing to do with such people.

Shown up by what we love

Leaders are shown up by what they love, which set of desires they are following – the desires of the sinful nature or the desires of the Holy Spirit. Whenever I am invited to teach trainee leaders about spiritual leadership, I always emphasize that:

- Godly attitudes are a higher priority for them than skills.
- Love is more important than activities.
- The display of God's glory in their character is the most important thing of all.

Only when we learn to lead with these priorities constantly in our minds will we grow as leaders.

> **To consider:**
>
> - If they were being absolutely honest, how would the people who know you well describe your character and attitudes?
> - What would they be positive about?
> - What areas would they flag up that need working on if you wish to continue to grow in being led by the Holy Spirit?

Leaders alight with a passion for God's Word

Returning to Dan, one of the other things nagging him was the oft-heard suggestion that growing as a Christian simply meant knowing the Bible better. Most leaders' bookshelves are groaning under the weight of commentaries and Bible study aids. However, as I look round my study, I can't avoid acknowledging the fact that, over the years, I have read a lot more books on understanding the Bible than on how to apply and live it.

James exhorts us not to confuse simply knowing what the Word says with acting upon it:

> Do not merely listen to the word, and so deceive yourselves. Do what it says. Anyone who listens to the word but does not do what it says is like a man who looks at his face in a mirror and, after looking at himself, goes away and immediately forgets what he looks like.
> (James 1:22–24)

Here are two of my convictions about the Bible and leadership:

- The Bible is the pre-eminent way through which the Holy Spirit speaks to us. It is impossible to be gifted by the Holy Spirit to be a spiritual leader without a deep and growing desire to be a Bible-centred, Bible-teaching, Bible-applying leader. To say, 'I love God but don't have much desire for God's Word' is as ridiculous as saying, 'I love my wife but I'm not interested in what she says.'
- The critical thing in leading and growing biblical disciples is to help them know what the Bible says *and* to live it out. To say, 'I love God's Word but don't put it into practice' is as ridiculous as saying, 'I love it when my wife talks to me but I'm not interested in doing anything she asks.'

The goal of leading people into the Scriptures is so that God will reveal himself and his truth, setting hearts on fire, and make people alive to himself and eager to do what he says.

Listen to how the psalmist describes his experience of what God's Word is meant to do to us:

- I open my mouth and pant, longing for your commands (Psalm 119:131).
- I rejoice in your promise like one who finds great spoil (v. 162).
- I long for your salvation, O Lord, and your law is my delight. Let me live that I may praise you (v. 174).
- I delight in your commands because I love them. I lift up my hands to your commands, which I love (v. 47).
- My soul is consumed with longing for your laws at all times (v. 20).
- The law from your mouth is more precious to me than thousands of pieces of silver and gold (v. 72).
- How sweet are your words to my taste, sweeter than honey to my mouth (v. 103).

You get the idea! This man is meeting God in his Word, exposing his heart to God, and God to his heart, and abandoning himself in worship. He hides God's Word in his heart so that he will adore God and follow him in joyful obedience:

> Your statutes are my heritage for ever;
>   they are the joy of my heart.
> (Psalm 119:111)

It is impossible to have a heart that is happy in God without enjoying the Bible, impossible to have sustaining delight in the Lord and to lead others in it without delighting in the Scriptures. But it is also impossible to continue enjoying him if we don't follow what he says. Jesus regularly told the Pharisees that their minute knowledge of the Scriptures was worthless because they didn't live it out.

> **To consider:**
>
> - What things most help you to enjoy the Bible?
> - What things hinder your enjoyment of the Bible?
> - What are the main challenges for you when it comes to turning knowing the Bible into doing what it says?

Warped Bible-reading

Unless our goal as leaders is to know and apply the Bible and have a heart that delights in God, we can easily fall into one or more of several dangers:

- We can think we are mature simply because we are educated in the Bible, rather than because we love and obey it. Knowing what the Bible says is never an end in itself.
- We can be tempted to assume that, when we have passed on what the Bible says, the job is done. But it isn't, not until everyone is obeying God and putting their lives under the Bible's authority.
- We can be tempted to substitute Bible studies for real discipleship. For example, faced with a choice between attending a home group Bible study that is comfortable and interesting (but non-challenging and unapplied) or spending an evening trying to share Jesus with a neighbour, many gravitate towards the study. We feel we have participated in a 'spiritual' activity, even though it may not have helped us to grow at all.

My top tip: Worship over the Bible

God is not glorified by Christians merely reading the Bible and knowing what it says. Nor is he glorified by leaders who merely teach accurate content, as they would from a textbook on any other subject. My number one tip for anyone who wants to be a Bible-centred leader is this: worship God over the Bible as you read it. Pray over it. We are meant to be exposing our hearts to God so that they exult in him and are delighted to obey. The whole point of reading and teaching the Bible is so that God receives worship in your life, and through you in the lives of others.

Teaching the Bible

When leaders teach God's Word:

1. God's reality is displayed so that his all-supremacy is seen and rejoiced in.
2. God's truth is presented so that people will be amazed at him.
3. God's actual words are spoken so that his reign is extended in people's hearts, wills and affections.
4. The good news of peace with God is proclaimed so that his enemies may submit, be forgiven and come into his family.
5. God's ways are understood so that Christians are edified, trained, corrected, rebuked, directed and equipped to follow.
6. God is shown to be our greatest treasure so that hearers will love him more than life and give up everything for him.

These aims should shape how we set about teaching the Bible. Here are some questions that I ask when I am reading the Bible with a view to teaching it. I ask these to help me get the Bible under my skin, so that I will live it out:

1. What did this Bible passage say and mean to its original recipients?
2. What was it written in order to achieve? God has put it here for a purpose, so what was that purpose and how does it apply to me today?
3. How does this part of the Bible produce faith and worship in my heart?
4. Am I going to pursue God for himself and be keener to get into his purposes for the world as a result of reading this part of the Bible?
5. Will I cast myself on God as my Lord and King as a result of this passage, or is it just a comprehension exercise? Am I stirring up my heart to be happy in him as I read? Are there songs I can sing to him, or about him, that are put in my heart by my reading?
6. Am I doing, or enjoying, the goal this passage was written to achieve (see 2 above). If not, then why not?

The wellspring for a leader's ability to work with other people for their joy in God is a deep desire to bring every area of life into delighted submission under God's Word. When a leader is hungering for God's Word, he or she pores over the Bible as regularly as possible in order to marvel at and worship him.

As I write this, I am praying that God will ignite a greater desire for his Word in your heart. Whether you have been a leader for years, or are just starting out, I pray that you will put this right at the top of your priorities. If you are presently tempted to neglect the Bible, or to use it to teach others while not enjoying it yourself, I pray that you will hear this wake-up call to sink your roots deep into it. The Bible is the source of our life, and the only firm basis for all godly spiritual leadership.

> **To consider:**
>
> - Do you regularly worship over the Bible? If not, why not?
> - Is your current experience of the Scriptures one of amazement and wonder? If not, can you identify any hindrances? Who might be able to help you recover your joy in God's Word?
> - Are you currently expecting Bible teaching to set people's hearts on fire for God and his truth? If not, why not?

6. CARING FOR YOURSELF AS A LEADER

Main principle: A well-nourished spiritual life is the bedrock for spiritual leadership

---

A challenging meeting with Julie

I had been a junior leader for less than a month when I wrote my first prayer letter. A couple of days later I met Julie, one of my prayer support team, in the high street. She said something I have never forgotten: 'I read your prayer letter yesterday and have prayed all the way through it. But there was something I expected to find that was missing.'

I asked her what it was. With the utmost kindness she said, 'You told us all the good things and everything that was going well, but you didn't mention any of your failures, things that had gone badly or mistakes you had made. Were you trying to cover those up? I would really like to pray about those as well.'

That pulled me up pretty sharply. Right at the start, I had fallen headlong into the temptation of wanting to validate myself by looking good. It wasn't that I hadn't made all kinds of mistakes, just not according to the prayer letter! And Julie saw straight through me.

Why become a hypocrite?

In Matthew 6, Jesus talks about hypocritical religious leaders who pray on street corners, let people know how holy they are when they fast, and give ostentatiously so that everyone knows about it. The reason they do this, says Jesus, is to receive applause from people rather than from God. He concludes that they have received their reward in full and won't get any from God.

I wonder why those leaders acted like that? Was it that they were insecure and wanted to be validated and affirmed, like me? Was it pride (like me)? Was it the culture of the day that wanted to put leaders on pedestals (like where I wanted to be)? Whatever it was, some combination of factors led them out of a private, God-centred spirituality into a public, self-centred spirituality. Maybe they had been taught that this was the way religious leaders lived? Maybe this had been modelled to them by others? Was it simply the way it was done?

But maybe there was a time when they hadn't been like that, when they had been humble before God, but, for whatever reason, that walk got eroded and then replaced with a veneer of holiness for public consumption.

People-pleasing

People-pleasing is a very easy trap for leaders to fall into. But it is spiritually lethal because it encourages us and others to judge our work by visible results, rather than by our hearts which we can't see. It is all too easy to let the desire to look good in the eyes of others control the way we lead. The first casualty for many leaders is our prayer life because people can't see that. When faced with lots of demands on our time, it is easy to persuade ourselves that activity is more critical than praying. Leaders are usually better at being Marthas than Marys.

Of course leaders are led by the Holy Spirit and a desire to see God's kingdom grow. But we can also be driven by the desire to succeed, the need to be accepted, pride, insecurity and the demands of others. When this happens, it is easy for us to stop being first and foremost disciples who are close to Jesus.

Add to this the fact that as leaders we work hard to care for others, often at the outer limits of our time and ability, but many people don't see a large portion of what we do. If we have neglected to nurture our souls, it can take just a tiny push to reveal our dark side. Maybe a person asks for one more unachievable thing, or someone grumbles about something comparatively minor, and suddenly we are laid bare.

'They don't know what I've done for them; they always complain,' is a symptom of not having been invested in ourselves, or of consistently living beyond the line of the maximum doable. It shows that our leadership capacity to absorb tension and help others make sense of life, God and the church has been eroded. It probably shows that we have spent more effort on being Christian leaders than on being Christian disciples. It can be all too easy for us to find our identity and acceptance in our leadership and the applause of people rather than in the Lord.

To consider:

- What factors in being a leader might hinder a person's walk with the Lord?

The destructive power of stupid pride

Here are some of my biggest struggles in maintaining a healthy inner life amid the demands of leadership, two of which we are already familiar with. We are going to focus on the final one:

- I become tempted to treat my spiritual life merely as work. I read the Bible because I want to prepare a Bible study, not because I am thirsting after God. Leadership quickly replaces discipleship. Projects replace prayer, and programmes become more important than people.
- I begin to believe that I am being godly because I am doing a lot. I start to believe that God loves me – and people will be pleased with me – because of the quantity of my work. I want to be seen to be doing valuable things in order to justify my keep or so that I can remain on a pedestal.
- Pride. I find pride comes easily because I am comparatively good up front and get to speak to large groups. I find it easy to believe in the myth of my own importance.

Pride is the main struggle for me because the default setting of my sinful heart is independence from God, not dependence and trust. It is the opposite of walking by faith. The devil loves to try to make us proud, because pride is the root of so much spiritual muck. Peter says that

> God opposes the proud
>   but gives grace to the humble.
> (1 Peter 5:5)

C. H. Spurgeon said that pride is a brainless thing and the

maddest thing that can exist.[1] It is certainly the problem most likely to overturn the spiritual value of my own leadership.

All this is part of being in a spiritual battle. Satan hates Christian leaders. He would love to replace our walk with the Lord with a holy-looking veneer. That is what was going on in Matthew 6. But the Bible says that God looks to the humble. Moses – one of the all-time great leaders – was the most humble man on the face of the earth, and God loved it (Numbers 12:3).

Finding soul-care

There is an unbreakable link between our life as leaders, our flourishing in leadership and our ability to run from pride on the one hand, and the care we receive for our souls on the other. Therefore it is crucial for leaders deliberately to prioritize growing with God. (I hesitate to say *more* crucial than for anyone else, because it is vital for everyone. But leaders can be more susceptible to the attacks of Satan than anyone else, and therefore in even greater danger.)

Taking practical, disciplined steps to develop and maintain a godly walk, with the help of others, is vital. Otherwise we will get ten or twenty years into leadership and find ourselves drained. This happens disturbingly frequently. If we want to grow the kingdom, and continue to grow ourselves in the Lord over the long haul, we cannot ignore the question of how we are fed.

> **To consider:**
>
> - Do you find it easy or difficult to receive nurture?
> - What are your current sources of soul-care? Are you currently being nurtured sufficiently?

Leadership snares

In the end, it isn't other people's view of our leadership that matters. This doesn't benefit (or hurt) us spiritually in any meaningful sense. But great gain comes from the 'well done' of God and from being content in Jesus.

Paul warns Timothy about a number of snares for leaders (1 Timothy 6):

- Failing to agree with healthy biblical teaching. Paul says this leads to conceit, but all too often people crave controversies and novelties.
- Money. Some people were peddling the gospel for profit, thinking that a veneer of godliness was the way to wealth. We should be grieved and heartbroken every time we hear about a leader who was caught with a hand in the offering plate, not only because of their sin, but because there was presumably a time when they were living uprightly and not falling into the temptation of money.
- Arrogance. This involves trusting possessions and wealth and self rather than trusting our God.

Let's not think we are immune. Timothy wasn't, or Paul wouldn't have warned him. Flee these things if you want to keep going with God.

Instead, says Paul, pursue righteousness, godliness, faith, love, steadfastness, gentleness. He says it is a real fight to reach the goal of faith, to keep growing in faith, and to keep burning brightly and strongly. It is a fight that we carry out by exercising faith. When we battle hard to keep the faith, more faith is the outcome. When we are saying, 'I am going to press after God and take hold of eternal life', he is working. He is our sustainer when we set about contending with unbelief and evil.

> **To consider:**
>
> - What things most help you to fight the fight of faith?
> - What most helps you to fight against sin?
> - What most helps you desire Christ and grow in godly attitudes?
> - What external input from others do you find most helpful?
> - How can you maximize receiving this right now?

Lots of friends to help

One of the things that Paul homes in on is the fact that Timothy made a good confession, with lots of witnesses. Pressing on in leadership is a corporate thing. We fight the fight of faith together. We are not generally very good at providing care for our own souls. So getting the care we need for ourselves from others is vital to our joy in the Lord.

The bedrock for Timothy is the deposit entrusted to him – the gospel. The foundation for his leadership is a lifestyle based on gospel convictions. According to 1 Timothy 6:12–16, the thing that keeps him firmly underpinned is not just that he has committed himself in the presence of many witnesses, but also that he has done so in the presence of God who gives life to all things, and Jesus who is coming in glory and majesty and might.

Helps for fighting the fight of faith

It helps me to remember that growing as a Christian in leadership is a fight of faith. If I expect life to be easy, then I readily become disillusioned and dispirited.

Here are three Bible helps and three practical steps.

Bible help 1: Stay in the vine
We want to be leaders who bear fruit, not those who wither and die. Jesus tells us very clearly how to keep bearing fruit: 'If a man remains in me and I in him, he will bear much fruit' (John 15:5).

Bible help 2: Resolve to know nothing except the cross
Paul says that he resolves to know nothing except Jesus Christ crucified (1 Corinthians 2:2). Even though he is feeling very weak and full of fear as a leader, the cross-centred message comes with a mighty demonstration of the Holy Spirit's power.

There is nothing like contemplating the cross for keeping us humbly close to God. It stops us being self-absorbed and opens the sluice-gates for grace to flow into us. Don't look for sustaining refreshment from any source that is divorced from the cross.

Bible help 3: Cast all your cares on Jesus
Jesus is willing and able to carry all our anxiety (1 Peter 5:7). Jesus himself says, 'Do not worry about tomorrow . . . Each day has enough trouble of its own' (Matthew 6:34). So keep praying prayers that release anxiety. In our culture, obsessed as it is with instant and observable results, I find this the easiest thing to forget. I would like to wave a magic wand and have all my cares suddenly disappear without me having to keep relying on Jesus. The command to keep casting cares on him is there to keep us continually dependent upon him. When we are facing hardship and difficulties that wear us down and sap our energy, he knows and cares. Let him be the first place, not your last resort.

Practical step 1: Arrange your lifestyle to make time for God

This may sound like an unusual piece of advice for Christian leaders. After all, isn't all their time devoted to being with God? You would be surprised. Many replace it with activities and meeting people's needs and responding to the demands of the congregation. We need our regular equivalent of Jesus going away to a mountain to pray. There is no easier way to burnout, ceasing to enjoy God, or gradually coming to resent the demands of leadership than a long-term lack of boundaries leading to no time to slow down and be alone with God.

Practical step 2: Be supported by your friends

Paul says that he has no peace because Titus isn't with him (2 Corinthians 2:13). (It is worth remembering, however, that he is exactly where God wants him to be. Just being where God tells us to be doesn't, in itself, guarantee peace of heart.) Later, he tells the Corinthians, 'God . . . comforted us by the coming of Titus, and not only by his coming but also by the comfort you had given him [to pass on]' (2 Corinthians 7:6–7).

Pursuing holiness is much easier with friends. Figure out how to respond to ministry situations with friends. Share the gospel with others together with friends. Worship and give thanks with friends. Get them to pray for you. Get them to partner with you. Share the bad things, as well as the good ones, with them.

Practical step 3: Make sure you are a worshipper

It's so easy for us leaders, whether old or young, to be so concerned about leading others that we stop worshipping ourselves. We have seen already how vital it is to maintain a healthy worship life. It is shown, for example by Paul's repeated command in Philippians to rejoice in the Lord, in which he emphasizes that worship is a safeguard for our souls. The way to keep in the love and joy of God is to rejoice with trembling:

> Serve the LORD with fear
>   and rejoice with trembling.
> (Psalm 2:11)

> Rejoice in the LORD, and be glad, you righteous;
>   sing, all you who are upright in heart!
> (Psalm 32:11)

> May all who seek you
>   rejoice and be glad in you;
> may those who love your salvation always say,
>   'The LORD be exalted!'
> (Psalm 40:16)

To consider:

- If your friends were able to look past your exterior and into your heart right now (as God does), would they conclude that they see a well-nourished spiritual life or a neglected one?
- What practical steps would you like to take as a result of reading this chapter?

7. YOU COULD BE A LEADER-MAKER

Main principle: You can learn to encourage and release new leaders

We should expect local churches to be the very first places where potential new leaders are identified and encouraged, yet comparatively few actively plan for this.

We're going to think now about how to spot, nurture and encourage new leaders throughout your church. Before you read on, you might like to pause to pray that God would raise them up. And, if you are daring, that he might stir up and equip you to become a leader-maker.

My friend Wanyeki is one of the pastors at All Souls in London, responsible for spiritual growth programmes. One day over a coffee I asked him what is his best test to know whether or not a believer is growing. Without hesitation he replied, 'Are they passing on what they have learned to others?' I think that is an excellent answer. Discipleship isn't complete until we are living out and passing on what we have received. It's not just about receiving more and more blessing or knowledge; it's about being a channel for the grace that I have received from God to flow to other people.

Let me teach you to do my job: James's story

This is equally true in the area of spiritual leadership. I once saw a great example of a church leader with a vision to multiply young leaders in his church. James gathered the youth group together one day and told them, 'In principle, there is no reason why you can't learn to do a lot of what I do. I want to teach you to do my job.'

He taught his teenagers how to pray, how to understand the Bible and give short talks, how to lead a Bible study group, how to explain the good news clearly to their friends and how to share their testimonies. They lapped it up and soon became some of the most mature Christians in the church, despite their ages. All it took was for one man to realize that you don't have to be a highly trained élite professional to take the first steps.

Leadership blockages

Do you remember Sarah in chapter 3? She didn't have James's level of know-how, but her experience illustrated that even a young, comparatively inexperienced leader can still be powerfully used by God to spot and encourage other potential leaders. Maybe it is too much of a stretch to say that all leaders have the opportunity to do this. However, it would be fair, for example, to explore with any church home group that has met for five years or more without seeing any emerging leaders what some of the blockages might be.

Here are five main hurdles:[1]

- Leadership blockage. This occurs when current leaders don't encourage new leaders. This might be because they don't know how, because they don't understand the need, because they are too overburdened or because they feel insecure about their own positions.
- Cultural blockage. This happens where the church is reluctant to accept new blood, is judgmental about failure or critical of unfamiliar patterns. No opportunities are given, therefore, for potential leaders to have a go in a safe environment. Trying anything new is simply too great a risk.
- Spiritual blockage. This occurs when a church isn't open to God giving gifts of leadership. We saw in chapter 3 that this is much more likely in the self-defined 'pastoral' community than in the 'missional' community.
- Historical blockage. The church has very defined structures and patterns for doing things. The pastor has always done everything, and that's just the way they like it. The church has never developed leaders before and can't think why it would be a good thing to do so now.
- No models of leadership development. This is where a church or its current leaders have no understanding of how leaders emerge and develop. It is therefore impossible to cast a clear vision for how to encourage potential leaders.

I want to be available to God: Thomas's story

Compare James's story with the situation Thomas finds himself in:

Thomas is twenty-four. He graduated three years ago and has since been working in commerce. From his late teens, he has been excited about the idea of church planting and would like to devote all his time to training towards this goal. Many friends and church elders agree that God may well be leading him in this area.

In a conversation with the church elders, Thomas wonders whether they could help him to start exploring how to teach the Bible.

'Could I spend some time with an elder learning how to lead a Bible study?' he asks.

'We don't really have anyone who would be a good trainer,' he is told. 'Perhaps you should go on a conference.'

'How about letting me have an opportunity to try giving a talk? I used to give evangelistic student talks at college and felt that God might be giving me speaking gifts.'

'We're sorry,' the elders say, 'but the speaking here is reserved for the recognized church leaders. We're sure you understand – it's a formidable responsibility and we wouldn't want anyone publicly teaching God's Word who hasn't been well trained. And the congregation demands a high level of teaching and wouldn't want an amateur doing it.'

'Well, how should I go forward in exploring how God wants me to use my life?' asks Thomas.

'The way it normally happens in this church is that we, as leaders, affirm that God seems to be leading a person towards ministry, and that person goes to Bible college. You would need to have saved the necessary money to allow you to go. The fees are around £4,000 a year, and you would need another £10,000 to live on. Say a total of £50,000 over the three years.'

Thomas is aghast. 'But I don't have anything like that kind of money. I still have student loans to pay off. And Diane and

I have been thinking about getting married. That would leave us without any possibility of getting on the property ladder.'

'Well, that is the normal route into leadership. We know that it carries significant financial burdens, and there are lots of sacrifices to be made. If the money makes it impossible, perhaps it would be better for you to think about it again in five years' time. Or perhaps Diane would be prepared to support you through college?'

'But all I want to do is start to have a go,' Thomas pleads.

To consider:

- How would you describe this approach to developing young leaders?
- What unreasonable hurdles is Thomas encountering?
- How would you help Thomas?
- Pause for a moment to consider what might hinder the emergence of new leaders within your church. Do you identify with any of the five hurdles listed above? If so, why are these particular issues in your church?

Looking for apprentices

Sadly, Thomas's situation is all too common. All he wants is to learn and grow, and yet no-one is willing to help him. It is quite possible that God is giving him gifts to serve the church – after all, God seems to have given him a desire to do so – but the church isn't set up to allow him to explore them.

Thinking back to the story of Sarah, the thing she did particularly well was that she looked for people to be her apprentices. Every Thomas needs a Sarah. Lying behind Sarah's apprentice hunt was an expectation and prayer that God could use even her. After a while, she really got into her stride, learned a lot of lessons, and leader-making became more and more normal. If Sarah was writing this paragraph, she would tell you that you too could do what she did.

Seven simple steps for raising leaders

Home group leaders, Sunday school leaders and others who grow further new leaders often report that they see God work when they follow some simple principles:

1. They pray regularly that God will raise up new leaders, especially that he will grow leaders who lead better than they do.
2. They are always on the lookout for embryonic leadership potential. This, of course, means knowing what to look for.
3. After checking with the main leaders of a church, they approach possible new leaders to talk and pray about how they might have a go.
4. They take the new leaders along with them. They teach, model and explain what they do. The new leaders become apprentices, just like Timothy with Paul.
5. They ease new leaders into opportunities to develop skills where God's leading can be confirmed in gentle ways.
6. They support and encourage new leaders as they explore. They lift them up when they fall down. They carry on feeding them as they pick up speed. They take responsibility, and protect young leaders from harm when they do something wrong.

7. They release them and cheer them on, praying all the time that the new leader will finally surpass them.

New Testament talent scout: Barnabas's story

We see a very similar pattern in the example set by Barnabas. I want to be like Barnabas more than any other man in the Bible, because of his spectacular gift of encouragement. First, he took Saul on as an apprentice and later young John Mark as well.

After Saul became a Christian, he tried to join the disciples. But they ran in the other direction as fast as their legs would carry them! We read in Acts 9:26, 'They were all afraid of him, not believing that he really was a disciple.' You bet they were! 'Saul? A Christian?! Not likely – it's got to be a trick. Just remember how he approved of Stephen getting murdered in broad daylight. We aren't going near him in a million years.'

I expect Barnabas was afraid too. But he did some digging around, found out about how the risen Jesus had met Saul on the road, and how he had then been preaching about him in Damascus. On the strength of this, Barnabas decided he was going to take a big risk. He saw the potential of God's grace and brought Saul to the apostles. Even as he was doing so, I wonder if there was a niggling doubt in his mind? After all, if he had got it wrong, they were all dead.

I have heard people say that they won't let potential leaders have a go until they are one hundred per cent certain that they won't mess up. But it is completely wrong to look for that kind of guarantee. It is a sure-fire way never to release any new leaders. By attempting to eliminate risk and failure, what we actually do is eliminate leadership gifts from churches. Barnabas, by contrast, was patient with failure. You can trace the story of how he took John Mark under his wing in Acts (12:25; 13:5; 15:37–40).

A little while later, in Acts 11, believers who had been scattered from Jerusalem to Antioch because of persecution started talking about Jesus to Greeks as well as Jews. It is hard to imagine now just how radical this very first cross-cultural evangelism must have been. When the Jerusalem church heard about it, they immediately decided to check out what was going on, and Barnabas was the best person for the job. When he arrived, he found evidence of the grace of God and encouraged all the new believers. We are told: 'He was a good man, full of the Holy Spirit and faith, and a great number of people were brought to the Lord' (Acts 11:24).

However, the very next thing he did was probably even more significant than his personal encouragement and evangelism in Antioch – he went to Tarsus and hunted out Saul. Having found him, he brought him back to Antioch where they spent a year together, meeting with the church and teaching large numbers. It was under his ministry that the believers were first referred to as Christians. Barnabas's first thought when he saw new gospel advances among the Gentiles was: 'I've got to get Saul. It would be great to have him here, and he would love to be involved in what God is doing with these people.' On the surface, the initiative to include this one man may not have looked very significant at the time, but it wouldn't be overstating it to say that Barnabas's apprenticing of Saul in Antioch was one of the great turning points in the growth of the early church and the worldwide spread of the gospel.

Finally, Barnabas didn't mind being surpassed. When we first read about his friendship with Saul, it is always recorded as the adventures of 'Barnabas and Saul'. After Acts 13:13 it becomes 'Paul and Barnabas' or 'Paul and his companions'.

Barnabas let himself fade into the background to allow the new leader to flourish in God's service. Another good example of this was when Jonathan, the prince of Israel, recognized David as God's future leader and graciously stood aside to let David take his rightful place in God's plans.

The pattern of encouragement

- Barnabas nurtured and encouraged.
- He took Saul with him as an apprentice and let him share his ministry.
- He let Saul take the lead.
- He let himself fade into the background.

What a good pattern of spiritual leadership development! But it is a hard pattern, and one that no leader ever follows if he or she fears other people surpassing them or becoming more prominent. And yet, whether we are home group leaders or youth leaders or lay readers or pastors, our constant prayer should be that, by God's grace, we might raise up leaders who are a hundred times more effective than we are, not so that we can take a holiday, but so they can break new frontiers and lead us further with God than we would be able to go by ourselves.

You can be like Barnabas

Barnabas was a spectacular encourager – hence the nickname 'Son of Encouragement'. Whenever I am invited to train leaders in a church, I like to joke that they should henceforward all think of themselves as Barnabasses. They are no longer home group leaders, but home group Barnabasses, no longer PCC members, but PCC Barnabasses. Barnabas just kept on and on encouraging. He gave richly out of his material possessions too, because he was more concerned with other people growing in Jesus than he was about the things he owned. He never missed a trick when it came to nurturing others.

You can be like him too. There is no reason for anyone at any age or stage in leadership not to be an encouraging talent scout for God. You might feel you are too young, but maybe you are in a better position to see what God is doing among your peers than anyone else. You might be much older, but more in tune with how to help people in their later years continue to grow in God as they press towards the finishing line. The critical thing is that you follow the seven steps above and know how to identify the marks of a potential leader.

The marks of a potential spiritual leader

> **To consider:**
>
> - Pause for a moment to write down how we might spot someone to whom God is giving gifts of spiritual leadership.
> - What do you expect to see in this person's character?
> - What do you expect this person to be passionate about?
> - What abilities do you expect this person to have, however embryonic these may seem at the moment?

Ferocious love for God: Michael's story

We were preparing to interview the final candidate for a trainee position at our church. The other candidates had done well, and we had all but made a decision. The final candidate, Michael, was the weakest, on paper.

'Let's face it,' said the pastor with ten minutes to go, 'he's going to have to pull something really astonishing out of the bag in order to get the job.'

First impressions weren't good. Michael was nineteen, by far the youngest and least experienced candidate. He was scared out of his wits, almost to the point of incoherence, and completely clueless about leadership, except for an unshakable conviction that God wanted him to learn.

He kept stumbling over our questions until we started to ask about his relationship with God. Then it was as if someone flicked on a light switch in him. Or exploded a bomb, more like. He got out his Bible and started thumbing the pages backwards and forwards, showing us passages that were special to him, enthusing about how he had been taught by his parents and how desperate he was to do the same for others. He was clearly thrilled that his sins were forgiven, and was frantic to learn as much of God as he possibly could. As we watched him for the next twenty minutes, his nervousness evaporated in the light of his ferocious love for God. By the end, he had us on the edge of our seats.

After Michael left, the three of us looked at one another. 'Well, that was . . . surprising,' the pastor said. And it was.

If we had had only paper qualifications to go on, we wouldn't have appointed Michael. And what a missed opportunity that would have been! He was an absolute handful to supervise and train because he wanted to know everything *right now*. He might not have known much when he started, but he was among the most teachable people I have ever met. My phone never stopped ringing, and the overheads in time and energy were high, but Michael has grown into a very fine young leader, preacher and fearless evangelist who is being used by God to reach people nobody else in the church will ever reach.

> **To consider:**
>
> - How willing would your church be to take on Michael?

God is *not* lucky to have me

Michael didn't have many marks of a potential leader on paper: no academic degrees, no previous experience, little immediately obvious talent, and not even a clear knowledge of where he thought God might use him – that came later.

The vital lesson for us as a church was that character, passion for God, humility and a desire to learn are far more important marks of a potential leader than are talents. And yet the world always tells us to look for talent first.

God doesn't sit in heaven saying to the angels, 'We up here in heaven are so fortunate that Marcus Honeysett became a Christian. What would happen to my great plan for reaching the world if we didn't have access to his talents?' I can pretty much guarantee that that conversation has never taken place! But it's just possible that one like this can be heard:

'You angels, do you see Marcus down there on earth? He is my child, and I love him. He wants to participate in what I'm doing, so I'm going to let him.

'It will be like when a small child asks his mother if he can help with the baking. The child doesn't help; in fact he gets in the way. Mum will have to clear up a huge mess afterwards *and* make the cakes all over again. But she loves the fact that her child wants to be with her to have a go. And I love the fact that Marcus wants to be with me. So I will let him have a go. Just look out for the mess he's going to make!'

Of course we shouldn't push the story too far. *Some* talent is necessary. And having an exemplary character alone doesn't make you a spiritual leader. There are many people of godly character with no leadership gifts at all. However, character always precedes talent. Talent without character may qualify you to be a leader in the world, but it disqualifies you as a spiritual leader in the church.

Therefore when we are trying to spot potential spiritual leaders, we are looking first and foremost for inner, spiritual qualifications. We should be looking for:

- A clear love for God and his Word
- A deep concern for God to be glorified
- A love for people and a desire to help others know and enjoy God
- Prayerfulness
- Servant-heartedness
- Kindness, wisdom and a spirit which is repentant and forgiving
- Ability to teach the Bible

At our Living Leadership training conferences, we teach the four fundamental foundations of all spiritual leadership:

- Living in the grace of God
- Knowing God's love poured into our hearts by the Holy Spirit
- A keen desire to grow in Christlike character
- Wanting to be a servant

Jenny, one of our trainers, often says, 'If I approach any particular area of life in asking whether I want to serve this time or not, I will always retain the right not to. If, however, I have decided once and for all that I am God's servant, that is the last decision I ever got to take. Subsequently, it is irrelevant whether or not I want to serve. I *am* a servant, so that is what I do.' For me, that gets right to the heart of the character of a spiritual leader.

There are other things we want to look out for too, but they always come in second place:

- Vision and direction
- Decisiveness
- Energy and perseverance
- Team skills
- Counselling or pastoral skills

What will it mean for you to be a leader-maker?

If you have read thus far, it is likely that you have already got a vision for working with other people for their progress and joy in God. Being a leader-maker is only a logical extension of this, as you encourage them to explore whether God is giving – or might want to give – spiritual leadership gifts to them. You are practically being a leader-maker already! The simplest way to discover if someone who seems to have the right marks might develop and grow into leadership is to try them out. You will soon see!

However, there are further costs to being a leader-maker:

1. We will need to spend the necessary time encouraging learners. Paul talked about 'fathering' believers, and that

is a good description of leader-makers. It is like being spiritual parents. They need our modelling, counselling, advising and intensive amounts of our time. It is impossible to parent young leaders without giving them a slice of your life.

2. We will have to give up things we enjoy doing in order to let others have a go. We shouldn't give new leaders the things we don't like doing, but the things we most enjoy. Almost by definition, they will start off doing them less well than we do. We will frequently feel that we can do things better ourselves and in a shorter time, but we will have to resist the temptation to snatch back the responsibility. Maybe there will even be times when other people in the church tell us how much they like it when we do things, but how much they dislike it when the new leader does them. Then we have to protect the new leader by taking the flack ourselves and not passing it on.

3. Sooner or later, we will get left picking up the pieces after some catastrophe. A basic rule of developing new leaders is that they get the credit if it goes well, but we shoulder the blame if it goes badly. And then, with some additional help, we let them have another go. While this is really hard, it is essential for building the next generation of leaders. And maybe God uses it to build grace-filled character in us too, that we would never otherwise enjoy.

Growing leaders is like having children. Sometimes they drive you crazy. Often they get things wrong. Sometimes they are over-enthusiastic or sulky. Sometimes they get sick on you when you feed them, but you don't stop feeding them! You smile and keep on feeding and encouraging them.

I would love you to get to the end of this chapter saying, 'I want to be used as a leader-maker by God.' I pray that your spirit will be stirred up by this. I would love to hear on the grapevine that your church is becoming a place where new leaders are regularly being identified, encouraged, resourced and released, in all areas of church life and among all ages. That would be a sure sign that your church is being effective for the kingdom of God. The need for spiritual leaders is the biggest need in UK churches (and further afield) at the moment. May God use you to help others take first steps in faithful and godly leadership.

> **To consider:**
>
> - How many of your church groups and activities have spawned no new leaders in the last five years?
> - Can you identify what some of the blockages might be?
> - Which of the seven simple steps for raising leaders given above are you good at? Which do you think require growth?
> - Are there particular areas of church life or spiritual gifting in which you especially enjoy encouraging others' gifts?
> - How good are you at including other people and letting them have a go at the things you most enjoy doing yourself?

SECTION 3:
How to look after your leaders

8. LOOK OUT – THERE'S A CLIFF!

Main principle: Every church needs to devote itself urgently to the task of growing new leaders

---

Everybody loves a cliffhanger. The hero's speeding car is heading for the cliff. The heroine is tied to the railway tracks in front of a speeding train. We sit on the edge of our seats holding our breath, and at the precise second that disaster looks inevitable, the action freezes and we are invited to tune into the next episode to find out if they managed to avoid certain death.

The reason why we all like cliffhangers is that they aren't real and we aren't personally involved. We are passive observers of the difficulties of others, and we are almost certain that, however bad the situation seems, the final outcome is going to be OK. James Bond never dies.

I want to tell you about a cliffhanging situation. Not a fictional one, but a very real one. Not one that we observe passively, but one in which every Christian has an enormous stake. A cliffhanger in which, from a human perspective, the outcome is not yet certain to be OK. The cliffhanger is that, in the church right across the UK, we are losing leaders at an alarming rate, the number of emerging leaders is falling, and the number of people leaving Christian leadership prematurely (from a human perspective) is rising. The average age of the main leader in most congregations is now in the fifties and going up, and the age of these leaders is often reflected by that of their congregations.

This is the reason why this book is so urgent. Within fifteen years lots of full-time Christian leaders will retire, and there won't be anywhere near enough leaders in the next generation to stay level. This is compounded by the fact that church sizes have shrunk to the point that the *average-sized* church can neither afford to train a full-time leader at Bible college nor has any skill at training them in-house. I strongly suspect that most average-sized churches are producing no leaders. Many churches that have always relied on external sources for full-time leaders and have no plans for developing leaders from within are very likely to discover that in the next generation their sources have dried up. By that point it will be too late for them to do anything about it. Where we see the trend being bucked, it is because churches and leaders have decided to put a high priority on enabling fresh leaders.

> **To consider:**
>
> - Why might current leaders not seek to develop fresh leaders?
> - What factors might put a person off exploring whether God wants them to grow into leadership – for example leading a home group?

- How much of your minister's time and energy do you think should be devoted to nurturing potential leaders?
- Is your church a place where potential leaders would feel safe to 'have a go'?

Hitting the comfortable plateau

I wish there was a simple, obvious answer as to why we see fewer and fewer emerging leaders. The busyness of living in a fast-moving world, the pressure on weekends for people with families at a distance, multiple leisure options competing for our attention, a sense that family activity comes before church, the seductions of money, all these things and many others play a part.

However, maybe the emerging dearth of leaders reveals that many people are reaching a plateau in their Christian life before they can consider becoming leaders. There is an instance of this in Hebrews 5 where the writer confronts those who ought to have grown into leaders and teachers but who preferred to remain spiritual babies:

> We have much to say about this, but it is hard to explain because you are slow to learn. In fact, though by this time you ought to be teachers, you need someone to teach you the elementary truths of God's word all over again. You need milk, not solid food! (Hebrews 5:11–12)

Apparently there was nothing to stop these people from growing into leadership except that they didn't want to put in the effort. They had reached a comfortable plateau early on and had stalled there rather than eagerly desiring to move on.

I couldn't do it . . . or could I? Dave's story

Dave is a friend of mine. He has been a member of his church for quite a long time, but never imagined he could ever be a leader. His home group leader saw potential in him, however. Dave didn't think he was very good at teaching the Bible, but it was obvious that he really loved it and wanted to grow as a Christian. He loved other people too.

When a gap emerged in the leadership of another home group, Dave's leader approached him. 'I think God has given you potential as a leader, so how would you feel about having a go? The leaders of the church will support and help you.' Dave laughed and gently declined, saying that he simply wasn't a leader. The group leader pressed him, however: 'At least you'll think and pray about it, won't you?' Dave agreed that he would.

A week later, before he replied, Dave went to see the leader of the second group to ask how he would feel about them leading together. When this man responded positively, Dave went to see the group. 'I'm not a great Bible teacher,' he said, 'but if you can cope with the fact that we will read the Bible and enjoy it, and learn from it together, I will come and try, if you'll have me.' When they also responded enthusiastically, he prepared and led the following week, before finally going back to his group leader and agreeing to step up.

> **To consider:**
>
> - What might cause someone like Dave to decline initially?
> - Describe the factors that made him change his mind.

This actually happened in the last fortnight. The thing I love about Dave is that, while he didn't quite see himself as a leader, he was at least prepared to consider other people's assessment of him. Being someone who was in love with Jesus, keen to grow as a Christian and willing to listen to others led him to take the initiative and explore further. Like Michael in the previous chapter, he has a profound desire to grow in God. If he hadn't been on fire, he would soon have found good reasons to decline.

Dave is not on a spiritual plateau. Plateaux arise when, for whatever reason, someone stops hungering for more of God. Maybe some people just don't realize that they are meant to continue growing all through their lives. They need a hunger for what God might do in and through them. Others have simply become comfortable where they are, and deliberately don't want to commit any more of their life to God. For them, we should be more concerned. They have lost their passion for God.

Spoon-feeding grown-ups

The people addressed in Hebrews 5 liked being spoon-fed. Just as infants need their parents to dish up sustenance for them, so these people wanted someone else to do all the hard work while they just received and consumed. But the difference was that they were adults! It is normal to see infants relying on parents to feed them. But when we see adults, who can easily learn to feed themselves, simply not bothering but expecting to be fed, there is obviously something wrong. They haven't grown up.

At some point all infants grow up and learn to feed themselves. It is the same spiritually. At some point a believer who is longing for God and thrilled with the gospel will learn to feed himself, wanting to know how to read and appropriate the Bible. He will want to know how to pray and give and sacrifice and serve and teach. He will no longer be happy relying on others.

The longer a person remains on the plateau of spiritual infancy, the more normal it will seem, and the harder it will become for them to grasp that there is more for them to enter into. The move from passively receiving biblical teaching from others to actively self-feeding on God's Word is the most critical step in getting off the plateau.

Don't teach me to fix teeth: Joanne's complaint

Joanne was approached by her minister. 'We are setting up a class for possible future leaders,' he said. 'We would love to explore with you whether or not God might have some future responsibility for you to take on in the church.'

Joanne politely declined. When her minister pushed a little harder, she told him: 'Actually I like coming to church just to receive and be fed. I hope that's all right, but I don't want to commit the time that your class would take up. And anyway, I don't think it's right to share responsibilities around like this. After all, that's what we pay you to do.'

The minister pointed out that his job was to equip and release everyone else to serve God, not to do everything himself. At this, Joanne started to get defensive.

'I don't see that that can be true. After all, nobody else has been trained like you have. You are trying to put important jobs into untrained, unprofessional hands. That would never happen in any other area of life, so I don't see why it should happen in the church.

'When I have dental problems, I go to a dentist. If I have legal needs I go to a solicitor. And when I have spiritual needs, I go to the church leader. I don't expect the lawyer to ask me to get involved in his legal practice or the dentist to offer to teach me how to fix teeth. I go to receive their services. Why should church be any different?'

Spiritual consumerism and traditionalism

Joanne is a spiritual consumer, someone who attends in order to avail herself of a product provided by others. She justifies remaining a passive receiver with her line about trained professionals. (I have actually had this said to me too!) Some people simply don't want to get off the plateau. They are too comfortable there and don't see the need for change. They will resist any challenge to go somewhere unfamiliar.

Today I was chatting with a rector friend on the phone. For several years, he has been extremely frustrated by having a large number of Joannes in his church. Today, however, he was upbeat. In the last few months, several new people have joined the church, and they are really going for it. They include ex-missionaries and a retired bishop. They are starting to help my friend drive forward with fresh direction and initiative.

'How are the Joannes finding this?' I asked.

'The level of resistance is mounting. I can tell we are doing the right things according to who is complaining,' he replied. 'I really think we have the ability to start going places, but I will need to find ways to survive the increasing level of complaints from passive consumers who don't want to budge.'

My friend really values church traditions, but not this one. 'They call themselves traditionalists,' he said, 'but what they actually mean is making sure they have everything exactly as they like and never hearing any challenge to grow with God.

I have told them that the most important 2,000-year-old Christian tradition is to love and obey what God says in the Bible, but that didn't seem to get through.'

These people sit under biblical teaching every week, but have a sufficiently impenetrable defensive screen to keep persuading themselves either that it isn't for them, or that they don't need to apply what is taught, or that it is simply beyond them. They resist the very changes in church life that are designed to help them go on with God. Needless to say, the greater the percentage of people who are in this category, the harder it is to get the church to think about developing any fresh leaders.

There is a million-mile difference between my friend Dave and the person who doesn't want to learn to fix teeth. They both sit in the same church services, listen to the same Bible, but one finds his heart racing at the thought of knowing God more and the other one doesn't.

Reigniting a passion for God

If hearts are burning with love for God, it is a safe bet that, with encouragement, leaders will emerge. There will start to be a regular stream. Wild horses won't keep them away from leadership. If many hearts are cold, however, then the result is likely to be Hebrews 5 spiritual babies.

How can we reignite such a desire for God that stalled believers start to grow again and new leaders subsequently emerge? Remember Paul's definition of growing in discipleship and maturity, from Philippians 1: 'I will continue with all of you for your progress and joy in the faith, so that through my being with you again your joy in Christ Jesus will overflow on account of me' (Philippians 1:25–26). Having joy in God *produces* strong faith. Enjoying God afresh gets people off the plateau, and therefore, we might expect, fuels the emergence of faith-filled new leaders.

Strong faith, flowing out of a joy-filled relationship with God, is a sure starting point for bucking the trends in leadership. And the great thing is that you don't even have to be a leader in order to make a difference – you just have to be an encourager. I believe that every single Christian is potentially an encourager. You can help change the mindset that makes people want to stay in a spiritual rut.

So whether or not you are a leader, you can be part of God's plans for leaders. You can be a Dave or a Sarah, and you can help others be Daves and Sarahs. Maybe as you are reading, you can already think of some people whom you could encourage to love Jesus more this week. Your church is the place to light the fire of fresh leaders. God can use you to be a heavenly firelighter!

> **To consider:**
>
> - Write down the names of one or two people whom you could encourage in this way. Take a few minutes now to pray for them.

Leaders grow leaders . . .

While everyone can play a vital part in creating a church that is on fire for Jesus and where leaders naturally tend to emerge, there is obviously a particular part that current leaders have to play. They are the key people for helping fresh leaders arise, because they have been given responsibility by God to train others.

Recently I spoke to an older pastor who told me that, when he became a church leader, he prayed that God would allow him to raise up one additional pastor or mission worker for every year that he himself spent in leadership. I asked him how the numbers were stacking up. With a smile he replied, 'I am ahead by one!' This man had a great vision from the Lord for raising up and releasing new leaders. As I thought about our conversation later, however, I realized just what an unusual vision it is. If you ask most church leaders what they most want to achieve, raising up and releasing a new generation isn't high up the priority list.

. . . but I don't

Five years ago, I decided to discover why this might not be a high priority. Every time I had the chance I asked leaders, individually and in groups, what prevents them from equipping new leaders within their churches. Over several years, I heard the same answers again and again. Some clear factors were revealed. Here are six of the most commonly repeated answers:

The six 'buts . . . '

1. 'Nobody at theological college said I had to'

By far the most common answer is that, when they trained at theological college, nobody taught them that it was their responsibility to be a leader-maker. Worse still, some have told me that they were taught that 'faithful' leadership means taking every opportunity oneself and deliberately *not* handing responsibility to others. One even said, 'If I delegate to others, it feels as though I have failed in my responsibilities.' Rather than understanding that every single Christian is a gospel minister, and that his own responsibility is to equip a whole congregation of gospel ministers, this man had it all upside down. He thought that he was the only one who worked for God, and everyone else was there to consume what he provided.

2. 'I simply don't know how'
Related to this, the second answer is that people simply don't know how to be leader-makers. Never having been taught it, they now don't have time to start to explore how to do it.

3. 'I'm too busy'
Over-busyness is regularly listed as a leadership-killer. 'I do seventy hours a week and my family never see me. Please don't ask me to bolt that on top of everything else I do,' numerous leaders have said to me.

4. 'My congregation doesn't want it'
Another common answer is that the congregation doesn't want their leader to develop new leaders. 'They tell me that I am the one who is paid to lead. They wouldn't want to be led by anyone who does it less well. And they wouldn't want to free up some of my time to disciple junior leaders because that would mean exchanging something for which they can see the short-term benefit for something that seems much less concrete.'

5. 'New leaders won't do it as well as me'
It is natural and understandable to worry about things being done less well, but when push comes to shove, that's how new leaders learn. However, I have sometimes wondered whether, underlying this, there is also another concern, which is that they might actually do some things better. A well-known church leader told me that, after one of his junior leaders had preached an excellent sermon, someone said to

him in the church foyer, 'There you are, Bob, you've just done yourself out of a job.' 'I knew it was a joke,' he said, 'but it still stung.' I know churches where nobody is allowed to exercise a level of gift or skill that is greater than that of the pastor. Such leaders never pray for a fresh generation who will be far more effective than themselves. However, it doesn't help for a church in this situation simply to blame the pastor for wanting to be in control. The question everyone should ask is, 'What is it about this church that makes our leader feel insecure?'

6. 'I don't want to try anything new'

'We don't like trying new things,' is the last reason. 'We are naturally cautious,' one group of senior leaders told me. 'Our congregations are cautious. We don't like trying new things without cast-iron guarantees of success first.' Unbelievably, the leaders who said this to me know that they are not replicating and multiplying themselves, but would rather not do anything that risks failing – or the disapproval of their congregations – than try new initiatives that might turn the situation around. Aside from the fact that the Bible tells us to walk by faith and not by sight, trusting God to bring about the results he wants, these churches are, humanly speaking, certain to wither and die because of this mindset.

I have been struck time after time by the fact that many leaders are fully aware that they are not replicating themselves at anything like the necessary rate. Some have told me that they even know people in their congregations who are gifted by God as leaders, but that they just can't see how to entrust responsibility to them and release them to have a go, or how to disciple and train them for the future. One leader said, 'Our educational culture doesn't lend itself to a problem-solving mindset. We are good at analysis, but poor at proposing solutions. I wish I was an American – they seem to be good at trying new things!'

Churches die when leaders die

What a counsel of despair is revealed in these six 'buts'! They tell us that large numbers of leaders know that there is a severe problem, but when push comes to shove they are likely to do nothing. They feel they don't have time, they don't know how, they have no energy. They will be resisted if they make changes, and they are full of fear that people won't like it.

It really doesn't have to be this way! How different is Lord George Carey's vision of leadership and growth in local churches:

> Churches die when leaders die. Churches die from the top downward. Show me a growing church and you will show me a visionary leadership. It is leaders who make growth. When you have spiritual leaders, men of prayer, women of prayer – imaginative, alert, intelligent – there we have growth.[1]

To consider:

- Which mindset does your church have? The despair mindset or the Lord Carey mindset?
- Which of the two mindsets do you think most churches have?
- What factors might lead a church into the despair mindset?
- Once there, what can be done to redeem the situation?

> - Do leaders known to you have any vision for raising up other leaders every year, in a similar way to the pastor mentioned above? If not, why not?

The elephant in the room

The emerging leadership crisis is the elephant in the room that most churches – and sadly many leaders – choose to ignore or not talk about. I doubt that you have heard much reflection on it in your church. And yet many churches are starting to feel the consequences, and will do so much more in years to come. Your church needs leaders, or will do very soon. And yet the matter is low on the priority list of most churches, when it ought to be right at the very top.

Every church needs a clear leader-development strategy, not just among the leaders, but wholeheartedly supported by everyone. Leaders can dream about developing others, but if the church as a whole doesn't think it is important or refuses to release a portion of their time, then it remains just a dream.

Leader-development strategy

What elements does a church need in a strategy for developing leaders? We might expect to see some or all of the following:

- 'Developing leaders' listed among the church's regular top prayer priorities
- The church and its officers taking steps to release a portion of the pastor's time to concentrate effort on encouraging and discipling possible new leaders

- Encouragement for the minister or vicar and others to receive on-the-job training in being leader-makers
- The setting up of a basic leaders' training course over the next year (appendix 3 has a list of subjects that you could include)
- Teaching that confirms it is OK to have a go at new things that may not work.
- A culture where embryonic leaders have a go, and the church is encouraged to love new leaders through their first baby steps and failures

Are the above found in your church? If not, why not? Is it that your congregation (or a significant percentage of it) are on a spiritual plateau? Or is it that you simply never think about the subject? Is it that you are rushing around with so many activities that it never makes it on to the agenda, or can you simply not see the elephant? Is it that you realize the severity of the issue but don't know what to do?

It may be difficult to set aside the necessary time to begin to address the issues and overcome the inertia. When we do, however, there is a gradual gathering of pace, first as we pull out of the stall, and then as the development of fresh leaders begins to snowball. When such development becomes normal, the effort required to maintain it diminishes because the church no longer needs convincing that it is worth committing the time and energy to it. The one unacceptable option is to do nothing at all.

9. HOW TO LOVE AND ENCOURAGE SPIRITUAL LEADERS

Main principle: Churches that actively nurture their leaders enjoy dynamic, spiritually fresh leadership. Churches that don't encourage leaders, don't.

Isolated and lonely: Peter's story

Peter is a Baptist pastor. For several years he has had a long-running minor disagreement with some of the church deacons about the way he uses his time. They insist that he has been employed by the congregation to serve its spiritual and pastoral needs. When he approached the deacons to ask if he could be released from preaching one Sunday sermon out of eight (eight hours a month including preparation), in order to free up some time to mentor two leaders in the youth group, he was told, 'We have employed *you* to preach, and pastor, because it is you we want. If you want to mentor people in addition, feel free, but not *instead of* other things.'

Recently Peter has also been struggling personally with some issues of doubt. He would love to have the chance to talk them through with someone who could help him resolve them, but he is fearful that his church might get to hear about it. The favourite catchphrase of one of the deacons is: 'What every Christian ought to be, our pastor *must* be.' If some of the pastor's internal struggles become public, he can't be sure that he won't be asked to resign his pastorate. This would leave him without a house or any means to support his young family. Reluctantly, he decides his only option is to press on alone, praying that the Lord will help him resolve his struggles in isolation.

> **To consider:**
>
> - How do you respond to the deacons' understanding of what they employ the pastor for?
> - What are some possible consequences in Peter's life of the expectations the church has of him?
> - Should he seek support from others, if there is a realistic possibility that the act of doing so will lose him his job?

Placed on a pedestal

I wish Peter's story was fictional, but it isn't. I have heard similar stories from leaders at all levels. The longer they have been serving, the greater the numbers who struggle with feeling overstretched, undervalued and placed on the pedestal of congregational expectations of sinless perfection. Needless to say, not only is Peter's story a recipe for leadership catastrophe in the future, it also makes it very unlikely that he will enthusiastically invest in bringing on the next generation of leaders. The church doesn't even want him to mentor the youth leaders.

Do churches work with leaders for *their* joy . . . ?

The work of spiritual leaders is to help disciples of Jesus make progress in their faith and have joy in God. However, if they are to help others, it is critical that leaders receive the same kind of encouragement. Their ability to do the job flows out of their enjoying God themselves. In the last chapter, we heard wise words from the former Archbishop of Canterbury, Lord George Carey: 'Churches die when leaders die. Churches die from the top downward.' Or, to put it the opposite way, churches flourish spiritually when leaders flourish.

Yet, as a general rule, most churches don't consider how to provide leaders with the level of spiritual encouragement that the leaders provide for them. For example, most members of most churches will have no idea who feeds the people who feed them, or even whether or not this is happening. They would be embarrassed to ask, so they assume that it must be happening behind the scenes. In very many churches this is an unwarranted assumption. The people doing the feeding are often the least fed themselves – with the exception of their spouses. (Ministers' wives regularly carry the highest burdens of expectation and loneliness in a church in return for the least support and care.) As Eugene Peterson, author of *The Message*, says:

> Far more activity is generated by [spiritual leaders] than there are resources to support them. The volume of business in religion far outruns the spiritual capital of its leaders. The initial consequence is that leaders substitute image for

substance . . . the final consequence is bankruptcy. The bankruptcies are dismayingly frequent.[1]

. . . or for their discouragement?

In my work with Living Leadership, I regularly receive mail from leaders telling me how hard the going is and wondering if it would be all right to jack it in. It's not that these people are averse to hard work and sacrifice. Most feel that they sacrifice more for God's kingdom than anyone else in their church, and they do so willingly (while wishing that others would follow their example and make the same level of commitment). The main reason is simply discouragement, often compounded by isolation.

Of course frustrated leaders are nothing new, and there are plenty of examples in the Bible. The people of Israel didn't want the leadership of Moses (or God). They wanted to be back in Egypt rather than in the place God had promised them. They preferred idols. Other leaders, including Moses' family, rebelled, and he faced constant low-level grumbling.

Nehemiah received continual threats, taunting and schemes to harm him. Opponents tried to canvas block opposition to his leadership. Isaiah and Jeremiah faced outright opposition from those with far greater power, from false prophets and false shepherds, all within the people of God. And the people tried to insist that Ezekiel should only tell them what they wanted to hear.

Even Jesus himself contended with fickle crowds who wanted him for what they could get out of him. In John 6 he made some demands which they found unwelcome, and went from having 5,000 followers to just twelve in the space of minutes. The apostle Paul experienced division over leaders (1 Corinthians 1:10), accusations that he was inconsistent, unreliable or a liar (2 Corinthians 1). He encountered people who loved a false gospel (Galatians), and endured suggestions of false motives (1 Corinthians 9: 'he's just in it for the money'), hurtful comparisons with other leaders who seemed outwardly more impressive (2 Corinthians 11), insults (2 Corinthians 12) and smear campaigns (Philippians 1:17).

Leadership-killers

One of the reasons why all this was written down in the Bible was to serve as examples and warnings to make sure that we don't replicate the situations in our churches! And yet we don't always seem to learn the lessons. Some years ago I started to make a note of the things spiritual leaders told me discouraged them – and the list just grew and grew. I call them 'leadership-killers'. I have listed them in appendix 4. It is a depressing read, but it would be worthwhile to spend a few minutes reading it now.

> **To consider:**
>
> - How many of the leadership-killers in appendix 4 might apply to leaders in your church?
> - How might you eliminate some of the discouraging factors?

It shouldn't be this way

The most regular leadership-killers seem to be:

- Isolation
- A spiritually stalled church

- Resistance
- Unrealistic demands, leading to an impoverished prayer and worship life
- Ego
- Worry
- Overwork, maintaining our standing in the eyes of others

The chief danger for those living with constant leadership frustrations and few encouragements is not that they immediately stop being godly, but more subtle than that. Leadership-killers more often work by emptying the spiritual fuel tank slowly and gradually. Leaders without any sources of encouragement tend, over a period, to put on masks and *pretend* to have a deeply God-directed life, rather than actually *possessing* a deeply God-directed life. A God-directed life is replaced with self-absorption or task-absorption, and wisdom and prayerfulness are replaced with whatever seems to make the job work. Every frustration is a temptation to perform acts of righteousness before people, to be applauded by them, as Jesus warned in Matthew 6.

The consequence, for many full-time leaders in particular, is that they end up distancing themselves from the community they lead, for the sake of emotional survival. They thought they would be in close fellowship, but find themselves exercising sacrificial love that isn't either recognized or reciprocated. They struggle with being the focus of every wrong expectation and piece of criticism in the church. They are spiritually drained by receiving all the blame every time something goes wrong. Perhaps the hardest challenge of all is when their credibility, integrity or trustworthiness are challenged. Some churches I know seem almost set up to drain leaders spir-itually and emotionally, a strong indicator that something is badly wrong.

You may think I am being alarmist. All I can say is that my experience of talking widely to leaders suggests otherwise.

How can we turn this around?

The apostle Paul told the church in Thessalonica: 'Respect those who work hard among you, who are over you in the Lord and who admonish you. Hold them in the highest regard in love because of their work' (1 Thessalonians 5:12–13).

The writer to the Hebrews says something very similar: 'Obey your leaders and submit to their authority. They keep watch over you as men who must give an account. Obey them so that their work will be a joy, not a burden, for that would be of no advantage to you' (Hebrews 13:17).

These are difficult passages for any spiritual leader to teach without sounding like they are demanding homage! But the unfortunate consequence is that many churches never hear what God says about how to help leaders flourish rather than wilt. And they also never get to hear that the church as a whole has a large part to play in helping leaders flourish. These verses tell churches to respect leaders, hold them in high regard in love, and obey and submit to their leadership, in order that their job will be a joy rather than a burden.

American pastor John Piper puts it well:

> A church should have a bent towards trusting its leaders; you should have a disposition to be supportive in your attitudes and actions toward their goals and directions; you should want to imitate their faith; and you should have a happy inclination to comply with their instructions.[2]

Churches are meant to ensure that the task of leading them is a cause for joy, not for depression. When people make life perpetually difficult and unpleasant for leaders, so that all the joy drains away, the repercussion is that the life of the church will also be drained of all its joy. Far from contributing to leaders being happy in God, the church will actually be working against it.

The most important question to ask

By contrast, where leaders find their task a delight, the consequence for the church is that it will be full of godly joy. Here is the single most important question that every church should ask at least once a year if it wishes to have joyful spiritual leaders: how can we honour and love our leaders as much as possible?

It really does make all the difference. I saw this in action in a mission organization I used to work for. We had a brilliant staff team who loved their work, but were constantly burdened by low salaries in the high-cost area in which we worked. While I had no power to increase their income, team members knew that at least once a term the associate team leader and I dedicated a day to thinking about just one thing: how could we best honour and care for them so that they would continue to love God, love people, love leading and love the ministry? We asked ourselves:

- How can we be as creative as possible in investing in their lives?
- How can we make them feel outrageously happy so that they are able to serve God as well as possible?
- How can we ensure they are enjoying God and receiving richly from his goodness?
- How can we help them be spiritually fresh and vibrant?
- How can we so encourage them that they will never want to be anywhere else?

The result was the strongest sense of teamwork that I have ever known. I get a warm glow every time I think about that team!

Mapping out the route: Nine signposts to encourage spiritual leaders

So what does the route map look like, the one that leads to flourishing, well-loved and well-nurtured leadership? How can we help leaders finish the race, still rejoicing in God and loving the task? Just as signposts can encourage you on a long car journey (viewpoint, toilets ahead, 10 miles to destination), I want to suggest nine clear signposts that chart a route into flourishing leadership. I will group them under four headings:

Spiritual care for leaders	No leadership-killers allowed
	Joy approaching
Opportunities for leaders to grow	Spiritual sustenance here
	Vehicle service and MOT available
	Viewpoint ahead
Real relationships for leaders	Families welcome
	Friends approaching
Correct expectations of leaders	Boundary line: Do not cross
	Pass 'Go'. Collect £200

Spiritual care for leaders

Signpost 1: No leadership-killers allowed
Hopefully this chapter has already helped you to consider whether there are any leadership-killing factors lurking in your church. Discouragement drains leaders like nothing

else. Satan loves to use it to make leaders shrivel up. If you have never asked the question: 'How can I help leaders to enjoy their work and enjoy God?', now is the time for you to start.

Perhaps the single biggest leadership-killer is the pressure of unachievable expectations. A church leader recently said to me, 'I cannot fulfil the demands made on me without working far more hours every week than is healthy for me or my family. The difficulty is that nobody knows how much work I do behind the scenes, confidentially, nobody knows how long it takes to prepare a sermon, and nobody has any idea how much time it is appropriate for me to spend praying. Many of the expectations are things that people shouldn't expect a pastor to do anyway. I feel that the workload is potentially infinite. I would challenge the expectations, except that that would mean challenging the people who pay me.'[3]

That leader is very likely to run on an empty fuel tank. He doesn't have enough time to do everything that is expected of him, but is unwilling to challenge the expectations. He will sacrifice his home life and probably his inner spiritual life in order to meet the perceived demands of the church, which always seem more pressing. But the church work won't necessarily be *good* work. There will be a constant temptation to live in maintenance or survival mode, in which the chief priority won't be extending the kingdom, but simply trying to keep too many plates spinning.

Leaders can make peace with leadership-killers simply because it feels like it would be too much of a battle to do otherwise. Therefore a key question for any church to consider is the following: 'Are the pressures and pace at which our leaders operate sustainable and healthy for them, for their families and for the church?'

Signpost 2: Joy approaching
The joy of the Lord is the Christian's strength (Nehemiah 8:10). Spiritual leaders find joy when they draw on God's strength:

> O LORD, the king rejoices in your strength.
>   How great is his joy in the victories you give!
> (Psalm 21:1)

It comes as no surprise that Paul repeatedly tells the Christians in Philippi to rejoice in the Lord. Rejoicing – actively giving expression to their joy in God – is a safeguard for their souls against legalism or trusting in their own strength rather than the Lord's. As we've already seen, worship – whole-life adoration – is central to being sustained in leadership. As leaders spend time adoring God, they receive from him. Worship is a great means of grace. As we read in Romans 5:17, those who receive God's abundant grace and the gift of righteousness reign in life. Strength comes from fixing our eyes on God and enjoying the fact that we are declared completely righteous in Jesus.

It is critical for every church to help leaders to be worshippers for themselves rather than always leading other people in worship. If one person leads or preaches at all your meetings, you should ask if this person would appreciate some opportunities for others to lead and minister to them. The state of a leader's heart is unfailingly revealed by the state of his or her worship life.

Opportunities for leaders to grow

Signpost 3: Spiritual sustenance here
Many leaders go for long periods without any kind of spiritual nurture. There is no guarantee that leaders feel as nurtured

in the local church as others do – although that is the biblical norm. Sadly, but unsurprisingly, leader surveys reveal that the longer leaders go without nurture, the greater the likelihood of their dropping out of leadership altogether through burnout, cynicism, apathy, compromise or sin.

The basic spiritual support structures for Christians are a loving, wise community; prayer; Scripture; rest and worship. Those are the soil in which disciples grow. Among the biggest causes of leadership failure is starvation on the part of leaders and their spouses of these basic, God-given means of encouragement. Continuing to grow in God as a leader requires thoughtful patterns of investment and care. Among the most crucial elements are:

- Regular patterns of support, whether through a prayer accountability group, conferences, retreats or some other means. There is no substitute for receiving love, grace and spiritual feeding from others in an environment of care.
- Extended time to devote to prayer and the Scriptures, both alone and with others, without feeling pressurized.

Signpost 4: Vehicle service and MOT available

I believe that, whenever God puts his hand on a person's life for spiritual leadership, it should be possible to assure that person that ongoing training, nurture and review will be there for them for as long as they lead.

Most leaders receive little objective observation of their life and leadership. Few belong to a sustaining, prayerful team of leaders. But just as it is good to get a mechanic to cast a knowledgeable eye over a car every few months, so having someone cast an eye over the life and work of a leader can create opportunities for God to repair, rebuild and recharge. I have been immeasurably helped as a leader by:

- One-on-one time with mentors who are more experienced than me
- An accountability group which keeps an eye on whether or not my leadership role is detrimental to my marriage
- Small groups of peers among whom there is honesty and transparency
- Team life in which leaders can sharpen one another's ideas and skills
- Regular access to training conferences
- Opportunities to pray and fast with other leaders at retreat days
- Individuals who phone me up to ask me how my leadership is going, and remind me who I am in Jesus

Some of these are easy to find, others more difficult, but I commend all of them to any leader who wants to continue to grow over a lifetime.

Signpost 5: Viewpoint ahead
There is nothing quite as refreshing on a long journey as a chance to get out of the car, stretch your legs and spend time enjoying a great view. Rest is godly and important, and uninterrupted periods are vital for energizing leadership. We might be able to carry on sprinting for ages when we are twenty, but our capacity to do so reduces with the passing years, even though our wisdom and leadership ability will hopefully increase.

Several friends have recently told me that they think that Sunday should be considered as a day off by their vicar. 'After all,' one reasoned, 'I work the rest of the week and participate in Sunday services on my day off, just like they do.' Anyone who thinks that Sunday is a day of rest for ministers has never been one! It is a wonderful thing to help others worship God and reflect on his goodness, but Sunday is definitely not a Sabbath for the leaders.

A businessman friend once said to me: 'If I see you working flat out in leadership all the time, I will stop supporting your work. If you aren't spiritually refreshed, enjoying God, spending enough time praying and reading the Scriptures and are constantly exhausted, then you won't have anything to feed me with spiritually.' That was a wake-up call. Building in rest stops and viewpoints is essential to growing as a leader over the long haul. God rested on the seventh day, and Jesus regularly went to quiet, remote places to pray. But I – and many of my friends in leadership – seem to forget too easily the value of days off, sabbatical periods, holidays, hobbies and opportunities to retreat.

If you want leaders in your church still to be growing in ten years' time, you would do well to discuss what will help them occasionally to take their minds out of overdrive, step back, reflect on what God has been doing through them, and enjoy the view.

Real relationships for leaders

Signpost 6: Families welcome
Do leaders in your church ever feel that they have to make the unenviable choice between serving the church or prioritizing their family? (The answer is yes, by the way!) Most leaders are aware that, at some time or other, they have been guilty of cheating on their family by being more conscientious about the church than they are about them. The demands of church are often clearer than the demands of family. Most spouses acquiesce, even when they wish they didn't have to do so.

It is easy for leaders to fall into a wrong pattern of thinking: 'If I don't spend time in this leadership activity, then something will fall apart', but not to reason the same way about family life. Family bears the cost of making leadership go smoothly. The right order is: God, husband or wife, family, church, outsiders. Not: church, God, outsiders, husband or wife, family.

Every spiritual leader and their family will feel valued when the church asks how they can ensure that family life is built up rather than damaged by the church. Speaking personally, my strategies include my wife having executive control of my leadership diary. She reports to accountability partners who 'help' me if I am working to the detriment of our marriage! We often consider my diary a term in advance in order to mark out time exclusively for ourselves, into which the demands of leadership aren't allowed to intrude.

Living Leadership organizes an annual Pastoral Refreshment Conference to provide nurture for spiritual leaders and their spouses. Every year we notice that a high percentage of churches are happy to send their main leader on such a conference, but don't see any reason to send the spouse. Yet leaders' wives are often the people who carry the largest pastoral and spiritual burdens in a church in return for the least support. In some cases, churches have historic expectations of leaders' wives that may be completely unreasonable. In the worst cases, leaders' families are considered public property. Some churches expect to employ a leader and get a second worker free. I recently heard of a church that complained to their bishop that the vicar's wife declined to run their women's ministry. The bishop wisely replied, 'In that case, you should stop paying her!'

A wise church places a high value on encouraging and supporting the marriages and families of its leaders. Leaders feel loved when their families feel loved. A common cause of leadership failure is not that the leader decides to pack it in, but that his spouse feels they have gone for too long being isolated, undernourished and unvalued.

Signpost 7: Friends approaching
My best man has a great question that he asks me: 'What sin are you into at the moment?' I feel completely safe with him and therefore (usually) don't mind telling him. Author Gordon MacDonald talks about having Very Draining People and Very Resourceful People in our lives.[4] VDPs are a net drain on our emotional and spiritual energy reserves. They sap our passion. VRPs, on the other hand, are people we draw energy from, with whom there is honesty, openness, spiritual accountability, advice, counsel and critique offered in love. They give us an opportunity to look at our sin patterns without it feeling like a threat to our leadership.

Leaders are not meant to be alone. Sadly, in some churches there is still a model of a sole leader who exists in friendless isolation, though thankfully this is dying out. Not only is it unbiblical, it is spiritually dangerous to a frightening degree. Leaders will flourish where they have deep, close friendships. Leaders give spiritual direction and counsel, help others confess and repent, and encourage people to draw near to God to receive restoration and forgiveness, so they need to have a context in which to receive these things themselves.

It is absolutely inappropriate for a church to deny leaders friendships of depth within the church, whether this happens through some understanding of the relationship between leader and church being 'professional' or through jealousy of leaders having 'favourites'.

Ask your church leaders who their close friends are and where they live. If you discover that they have few or none who live close by, then it may be that they feel inhibited by the church from making friends, but are reluctant to say so. You should pray and actively encourage them to make friends a priority.

Correct expectations of leaders

Signpost 8: Boundary line: Do not cross

In the course of a recent discussion, a church leader confided, 'A family in the church were upset that I couldn't attend a family function. They don't understand that what was possible for me when the church was 100-strong isn't possible now it is 200-strong. To be honest, I'm struggling even to remember names sometimes.' He was tempted to attend, partly out of love and partly out of guilt, despite the fact that it was clearly a request too far.

I used to supervise two leaders who found it nigh on impossible to draw boundaries and say no to people. The result was that they resented the demands placed on them by others – and, by extension, by God. They were drawn into an ever-upward spiral where they committed to more and more activities, and other people seemed content to let them do this. Soon they were both living with completely unfulfillable expectations.

I have thought about those two individuals often over the years, and have come to the conclusion that leaders are generally bad at setting healthy boundaries for themselves. They love what they do, and they love the people too. They rightly want to work hard, giving their lives for the glory of God. It is rare to meet a spiritual leader who is more tempted to laziness than to overwork. Success is not easy to define in spiritual leadership, as it is in other areas of life. There is no visible product or financial bottom line to measure whether leaders have a done a good job or not. Numbers alone are a hopelessly inadequate measure. The temptation therefore is for leaders to do more and more in order to feel that they have done enough.

A church leader in his early forties once told me that he was struggling with weariness and wondering if he might need a sabbatical. Even a cursory glance at his leadership patterns was enough to show that he had been labouring under massive and unsustainable demands for well over ten years. He had a high capacity for work, and in his position many others would already have disintegrated by then. But he was reluctant to raise the issue with his church. 'They don't get the chance for extended time away from work,' he said, 'so how can I justify asking them to establish boundaries for me if some of them work more hours than I do?'

This is a reasonable question, but it comes down to this: does the church want to have an energized or an exhausted leader? They may struggle with the idea that he or she may need to do less in order to stay spiritually fresh, but the alternative is leaders who are no longer full of joy. A wise church doesn't equate quantity of leadership with quality of leadership, and will actively help leaders know how to take time off, carefully setting boundaries when leaders themselves are unable to do so.

Signpost 9: Pass 'Go'. Collect £200
The final signpost relates to the way a church honours its paid leaders. Whenever leaders give up prematurely, it is common to find that their church expected them to work with unacceptable and dishonourable pay and conditions. I have talked to a distressing number of pastors and their families who feel that the church wants to get as much as possible, while paying them as little as it can get away with.

Don't expect dynamic spiritual leadership from those who are perpetually worried about money. Don't expect to pay church leaders so much less than the average income in your area that their children will never have the same advantages as everyone else's. Don't insist that they live in a tied house but deduct the commercial rental value of the house from their salary package. That will only ensure that they are never able to buy somewhere for themselves to live, and likely mean that they will retire in poverty.

Some churches are small and don't have much money. It is OK for such churches to approach a potential leader saying, 'We can't afford to pay a reasonable wage yet, but if you work with us, we will do our utmost to honour you and alter that as God brings growth.' What is not acceptable is a church effectively saying, 'You have a calling from the Lord, and we are happy to presume on it.' That is nothing less than an abusive relationship between church and leader, and it is ultimately responsible for a great deal of leadership failure. Treating leaders in ways that cause resentment is a sure-fire way to drain their spiritual vigour.

Honour leaders

This chapter has been about how to work with leaders for their progress in the faith and their joy, so that they will be spiritually fresh and energized to work with others. The underlying principle is very simple: honour those who do the work of the gospel. Paul tells Timothy: 'The elders who direct the affairs of the church well are worthy of double honour, especially those whose work is preaching and teaching. For the Scripture says, "Do not muzzle the ox while it is treading out the grain," and "The worker deserves his wages"' (1 Timothy 5:17–18). In other words, a church mustn't expect leaders (the ox) to lead well if they are deprived of the sustenance and support that they need.

I hope this chapter has given you plenty of thought about how to encourage leaders in your church. The church that regularly asks itself, 'How can we most honour spiritual leaders?' will have leaders who love the church, love leading and will never want to do anything else.

> **To consider:**
>
> - Are the spiritual leaders in your church feeling loved and encouraged by the church or taken for granted? How might you find out?
> - What one or two things can your church do as a result of reading this chapter, to better honour and encourage your leaders?

10. LET YOUR LEADERS LEAD

Main principle: The quickest way to destroy the vitality of spiritual leaders is to prevent them exercising their spiritual gifts

---

This chapter continues the theme of encouraging leaders so that they flourish, and specifically addresses one area of discouragement: when those with leadership responsibilities are prevented from exercising them.

Messing about on the water

Baptist minister Derek Tidball likens leaders to pilots on board ship.[1] The pilot serves alongside the rest of the crew, under the authority of the captain and ship-owners, to fulfil a vital function: navigation. Never is a pilot more necessary than when a ship enters dangerous waters. To protect the ship from harm and steer it to the right destination, the pilot has to be competent and gifted, but he or she also has to be listened to. The crew that chooses to ignore the pilot and do things their own way is likely to end up shipwrecked.

Think yourself into the pilot's shoes for a moment. How would you feel if you were ignored by the crew in dangerous waters? What would it be like to warn them that unseen rocks are ahead, but not be listened to? You would feel a rising dread as your appeal falls on deaf ears.

Or imagine that the crew prefers the security of being tied up at the dock, not going anywhere. The port is much safer than the dangerous high seas. The crew are content because while the boat might not be going anywhere at least it isn't sinking. However, neither is it completing its voyage, delivering its cargo or making a profit for its owner. You labour and struggle, appealing to the crew to fulfil their responsibility to the owner, all the while feeling that your skill and effort are pointless because the crew is ignoring or resisting you.

Now think of the spiritual leader who is responsible for setting course and steering a church (or some part of it). The church has a precious cargo to be delivered throughout the world – the good news about God. It is the leader's/pilot's responsibility to help the crew make a profit for the Master. Sometimes they will have to steer the ship out of dead water and into fresh winds, sometimes through danger, or the rough seas of cultural change when delicate navigation is required, for example as one generation gives way to the next.

Imagine what it is like for that leader, given responsibilities by God, not being allowed to exercise them by the crew. Just like the pilot, he will spend time consumed with anxiety, believing that his skill and effort are pointless. There are few worse things than having responsibility to carry out a task that you are prevented by no fault of your own from doing.

> **To consider:**
>
> - Would you say the culture in your church encourages or discourages leaders from leading? Explain your answer.
> - Ask your vicar, home group leader, one of your church's PCC members or deacons whether they feel that the culture of the church energizes or inhibits leaders from taking fresh initiatives.

Don't burden your leaders

There are clear examples in the Bible of churches that will not let the pilot navigate. The writer to the Hebrews urges his readers: 'Remember your leaders, who spoke the word of God to you. Consider the outcome of their way of life and imitate their faith' (Hebrews 13:7), and also 'Obey your leaders and submit to their authority. They keep watch over you as men who must give an account. Obey them so that their work will be a joy, not a burden, for that would be of no advantage to you' (Hebrews 13:17).

It is common these days for people to distrust authority. Biblical verses that teach the crew to obey and submit to leaders can be treated with great suspicion. It seems from Hebrews that this happened in the first century too. After all, what if leaders start to put on airs and graces? What if they manipulate and abuse their position? The pilot image is helpful. Derek Tidball comments that, while it is certainly possible to abuse positions of leadership with authoritarian*ism*, nevertheless:

> we cannot avoid the fact that the pilot carries real authority. True, it is only temporarily delegated by the master or officers,

but it is authority nonetheless . . . [We] neglect this aspect of the pilot's role to our detriment.

It is vital that the pilot should exercise authority; the task could not be completed without it.[2]

How to cripple your church

The implication of Hebrews 13 is that, when churches don't allow godly leaders to lead, their work becomes a heavy burden, in just the same way as for an ignored pilot. The fastest way to discourage and debilitate leaders is to prevent them from doing their job. Weighing leaders down like this, says the writer, is crippling.

Several months ago I wrote an article for a couple of Christian magazines on the reasons why some churches decline. I was completely taken off guard by the flood of letters and e-mails in response. They all came from leaders who believed their church was becalmed or heading for the rocks, but felt that they were prevented from navigating. In the worst case, members of a church said to their leader, 'We haven't changed for thirty years. We have seen off the last three leaders. We will sit you out too.' (Thankfully there weren't many of those – but even one is one too many!)

As more and more letters arrived, they revealed a picture of some of the main reasons why leaders may be prevented from exercising their role:

I want the organ-grinder, not the monkey

Imagine the shipboard pilot who knows he is there to navigate, but nobody has told the crew. They don't really know what his job is. In the case of pastors, the navigation of the church is done by biblical teaching. The largest number of leaders who wrote to me said that they had thought this was what they had been invited to do when they came to pastor their church, but after arriving, they realized that most people merely wanted someone to run their favourite activities and do pastoral visits.

Shared expectations about what a leader does – and how the relationship between leader and church should work – need to be clear from the start. It is critical that church and leader agree and share a clear understanding of the principles of leadership, what the limits of the job description are, and how church governance works (i.e. are leaders actually allowed to lead?). Unless there are such shared expectations, leaders inevitably end up shouldering extraneous responsibilities that they shouldn't, eroding the time they have available for what they should be doing (like training new leaders).

It is also vital that a church knows when their leaders should lead by consensus and when they shouldn't. Leaders should lead by consensus wherever possible, for example on matters of how to fulfil particular practical aims. But there are times when a more autocratic decision is necessary; for example, leaders *cannot* lead by consensus on matters of doctrine. It is then that they have to know they will have the unqualified support of other leaders and the church.

There will also be times when expectations need to be reviewed. The church I am a part of has grown past 200 on a Sunday. We will shortly need to review our expectations of our pastor because a leader who was able to know everyone and be involved in everything when there were 100 people can't do the same when there are 200 plus. The church needs to accept that our pastor can no longer do everything they valued when the church was smaller, if we are to continue to see further growth.

Unless we review this carefully, there will be constant pressure on our leader to do all kinds of really good things that are not central to the job. (And I am often surprised at how regularly churches underestimate the monthly hours their leaders spend on the job, or how little comprehension there is about how long various aspects of the work take.) Attending every meeting, preaching every sermon, visiting every needy person and answering every e-mail personally may seem like a valuable use of time at first glance, but this will ultimately cause a church to stop growing as the leader's capacity dwindles. A leader told me that a woman in his church had said to him, 'It isn't a proper pastoral visit unless it is done by the pastor. I don't want anyone else – I want the organ-grinder, not his monkey!' Her emotional appeal was designed to get the leader to respond by making him feel guilty, but it was driven entirely by a narrow view of her own needs, rather than the wider needs of the church.

It is always better to be careful . . .
Another set of letters revealed leaders struggling with how their church puts checks and balances on any new initiative. Don't mishear me, all leaders need to be accountable to the church, but often churches drift and flounder because the checks are so strong that they cause inertia. In Baptist and independent churches, for example, it is common to require a high measure of congregational agreement before doing anything new, which can result in a comparatively small percentage of people being able to stop anything they don't like. One leader told me that, when he began pastoring such a church, the congregation required 80% agreement to initiate or change absolutely anything. '5% would always resist everything, regardless of what it was,' he said, 'and bully another

15% into agreeing with them. A tiny minority had the whole congregation over a barrel.'

A gospel-driven church will regularly want to review its structures and mechanisms to see whether they are helping to extend God's kingdom in the world or hindering it. Leaders flourish when vision is warmly welcomed and when the normal tendency is to receive it with enthusiasm.

If the *automatic* response to fresh ideas for how to spread the good news is cautious, this shows that the structures need to be carefully looked at. Church procedures are meant to release, not inhibit, gospel initiatives. At its worst, this inertia (often under the guise of carefulness) simply enshrines a lack of willingness to walk by faith or take risks for God. People use rules and regulations as a comfort blanket to avoid anything they find difficult. In churches where such caution prevails, it is common to find frustrated leaders.

We don't trust you – give us Wikipedia!

Several leaders wrote with heartbreaking stories about congregations who simply won't trust them, regardless of how they try to prove their integrity and trustworthiness. The authority of the pilot is dependent on his or her credibility and reliability, which means that there are few quicker ways to cause a leader anguish than by casting doubt on their integrity. Read 2 Corinthians to see this in action. The whole letter consists of Paul agonizing: 'Let me lead you as I should – and as you should.' Sadly, it seems there are situations where the few who don't trust leaders make their feelings known, while the many who do say nothing.

Others said that they are regularly compared (unfavourably) to a congregation member's favourite internet preachers and gurus. If you want to find someone who agrees with you and disagrees with your church leaders, then you are certain to be able to do so online. One leader said, 'Everyone now wants to lead, and everyone feels able to challenge me like never before because of the internet.' In this day and age, authority is rarely vested in a role (like the minister). In fact our culture encourages everyone to be their own leader.

We liked the last person better

The last set of letters came from leaders who were drained by constant opposition. Some were being abused. Others revealed that there were areas of church life that were impossible to challenge or change without fear of being sacked.

We don't have space to explore the dynamics of disagreements, relationship breakdown, how arguments escalate, or how persuading with truth can be replaced by confrontations motivated by power. However, what struck me repeatedly in these letters was how easily Christians can express our opinions without kindness, particularly towards leaders. I didn't have firsthand knowledge of the situations of many of those who wrote to me, so don't know the rights and wrongs, or how things had become so bad. But I do know that, regardless of the specifics of conflict and confrontation, God has commanded us to love one another and to do our best to have the same attitude as Jesus. We can be ever so right, and at the same time ever so wrong, if we lack humility, kindness, servant-heartedness and grace. Disagreeing with leaders can be done two ways: with godliness and honour, or with ungodliness and disrespect. The first is actually positive, the second always destructive.

> **To consider:**
>
> - What consequences are these frustrations likely to have on:
>   - The personal life of a leader?
>   - The leader's walk with God?
>   - The life and growth of a local church?
> - How would you advise a leader who is experiencing one or more of the above to respond?

Running on empty

Whenever I meet a worn-down, burnt-out Christian leader, I give odds of 10 to 1 that they feel criticized, resisted or expected to put up with poor employment conditions. Or their spouse does. It is likely that they feel that their godly hopes and dreams are squashed rather than embraced. The work has stopped being a joy and the light has gone out in their eyes. They wanted, as did the apostle Paul, to love their people with the affection of Jesus, but found that that affection was spurned. Leaders have spoken to me about trying to shepherd sheep who steadfastly refuse to be shepherded, building a spiritual building with bricks that don't want to fit together, parenting a congregation that doesn't want to be fathered and mothered to maturity, and giving their affection, concern and love to those who refuse to receive it.

There is a very close link between spiritual energy and the ability of leaders to bring on new leaders. When the light in the eyes is extinguished, a leader is no longer capable of doing this. In fact, he will feel threatened by new leaders. And why would a new leader want to stick his head above the parapet?

If their impression is that leaders are rarely able to exercise their gifts and responsibilities to the full, leading becomes an unappetizing prospect.

Isolation, worry, exhaustion, lack of enthusiasm, the wearing of masks, and despairing of ever being able to exercise the gifts God has given, are far too common for many leaders. I wish these things never happened at all. In fact, they occur all too frequently. Over a period, initiative and godly vision will be replaced by merely doing what people want. Joylessness in leadership frequently produces a bunker mentality, and a growing professional distance between the leader and the community.

Spiritually fresh leaders

I have kept this chapter deliberately short because it boils down to one simple question: do you want to have spiritually fresh leaders in your church? Such leaders are critical to the health of spiritually fresh churches. But where they are crushed, you see churches heading for the rocks.

Hopefully your answer is a resounding YES! If so, there is only one more question for you to ask: how can I – and my church – make the task of leadership a joy rather than a burden? Lack of willingness to let leaders lead, and to trust and follow, is the ultimate 'freshness-buster'.

> **To consider:**
> Is your church likely to encourage or discourage leaders from leading?
>
> - Are the leaders expected to do everything and attend every meeting?

- Are the leaders overburdened to the point where they are continually tired?
- Do leaders bear the burden alone or with a supportive team?
- Is the normal tendency to trust or distrust leaders when they propose new initiatives?
- Do people publicly criticize leaders when they take difficult or controversial decisions?
- Are any salaried leaders paid an honourable amount for the work they do?
- The apostle Paul warns the younger leader Timothy that he will meet some or all of the following as he leads. Are any prevalent in your church?
  - People who like to oppose
  - People who are divisive
  - People who enjoy controversy
  - People who don't follow and obey biblical teaching
  - People who quarrel about minutiae and make mountains out of molehills
  - People who gossip
  - People who want to teach things that aren't in the Bible
  - People who don't like young leaders
- How can you encourage and honour those whom God has put in positions of leadership?

CONCLUSION: SPIRITUAL LEADERSHIP TO THE GLORY OF GOD

Main principle: Leaders use their spiritual gifts to build and equip a God-glorifying people

---

The apostle Peter gives his own amazing definition of church in his first letter:

> As you come to him, the living Stone – rejected by men but chosen by God and precious to him – you also, like living stones, are being built into a spiritual house to be a holy priesthood, offering spiritual sacrifices acceptable to God through Jesus Christ. For in Scripture it says:
>
> > See, I lay a stone in Zion,
> >   a chosen and precious cornerstone,
> > and the one who trusts in him
> >   will never be put to shame.
>
> Now to you who believe, this stone is precious. But to those who do not believe,

> The stone the builders rejected
> has become the capstone,

and,

> A stone that causes men to stumble
> and a rock that makes them fall.

They stumble because they disobey the message – which is also what they were destined for.

But you are a chosen people, a royal priesthood, a holy nation, a people belonging to God, that you may declare the praises of him who called you out of darkness into his wonderful light. Once you were not a people, but now you are the people of God; once you had not received mercy, but now you have received mercy.

(1 Peter 2:4–10)

Built into a spiritual house

Let's recap a bit. God is building Christians into a spiritual house. Elsewhere in the Bible, it says that we are a household and temple in which God lives by the Holy Spirit (Ephesians 2:19–22). Churches are amazing! They are not human organizations, they are spiritual communities. Peter says that these communities offer spiritual sacrifices, which means worship and witness in every area of life.

This is what God chose us for. He set his love on us. He wants a kingdom of priests (that is, all Christians bringing him glory from all over the world). The identity of a local church is completely defined by a passion for God's glory. Everything about a church is meant to be utterly God-centred.

We aren't just *defined* by God, we are also called to live *for the praise* of God. When we are built into God's household, we are given an invitation to offer to the world: 'Come and be part of God's house. Get to know and worship the King of the universe and become joined to his infinitely precious Foundation Stone, Jesus Christ.' This neatly sums up the purpose of every local church in just six words: *to praise him to the world*.

Spiritual amnesia

When things go wrong in a church, or when believers are simply settling for a quiet life rather than adventures with God, the first question to ask is: have we forgotten who we are? When we forget that we exist to declare to the world that God is wonderful, then we stop being completely God-centred. Our activities and our message instead become human-centred. We start to expect the church to be about meeting *my* needs, rather than about getting into the purposes of God.

When churches forget who they are, it is very likely that the leaders have forgotten who they are too. When leaders get amnesia about God's purpose for his church, when they no longer consider every day how glorious it is to be part of the bride of Jesus Christ, or when they stop thinking about how to participate in growing God's kingdom, their church defaults to happy, but spiritually mediocre, meetings and activities. These please the regulars, but are rarely life-changing. There is little challenge to explore new frontiers for God.

When a church heads into spiritual mediocrity, it is usually due either to a failure of leadership or a failure to follow godly leaders. Do you remember how Moses, Aaron, Joshua and Caleb pleaded with the people of God to follow God into the Promised Land (Numbers 13)? When the people refused, the result was forty years in the desert. Out of countless thousands, only two ever received the blessing. They could all have had it there and then, but they disconnected themselves from God's leaders and refused to follow their lead.

Being in God's team

If you had to sum up the purpose of your church in just one word, what would it be? Mine would be *growth*: the spiritual growth of individuals, growth in taking the good news to our area, and growth in the multiplication of disciples. Growth in the worship and praise that is being offered to God, and growth for his kingdom all over the world.

Our normal expectation should be that churches are life-transforming places where people mature as disciples as God's truth impacts on their lives. Every church should naturally be the place where people learn to grow in serving God, where they can be real with God and one another, and where they are encouraged to use their gifts as part of God's team. Churches are God's teams, spreading his glory.

But none of this happens by accident. Nobody drifts into spiritual maturity. Spiritual gifts don't develop all by themselves. Strategies for mission don't grow on trees. And team life and purpose don't just appear out of thin air. They all require deliberate action. When Paul talks about the body growing, in Ephesians, he emphasizes how critical spiritual leaders are in the process:

> [God] gave some to be apostles, some to be prophets, some to be evangelists, and some to be pastors and teachers, to prepare God's people for works of service, so that the body of Christ may be built up until we all reach unity in the faith and in the

knowledge of the Son of God and become mature, attaining to the whole measure of the fulness of Christ.
(Ephesians 4:11–13)

These leaders exercise this enabling, facilitating work by speaking the truth in love, stabilizing the church with correct doctrine, teaching and witnessing to the true teachings of Christ.

A person becomes mature when he or she displays that God is working in them, giving them the hope of glory (Colossians 1:27). The job of leaders is to help Christians fix all their hopes, ambitions and decisions on God being honoured. And to encourage not-yet-Christians to honour God as well.

Making Jesus look great

Every church activity you help lead – young people's group, the PCC, providing refreshments after services, pastoring, home groups – exists to bring God glory through helping participants to live as mature disciples. Leaders exist for others' spiritual health.

In a very beautiful verse, Paul tells Titus that slaves should be trustworthy and behave honestly towards their masters, *in order to make the teaching about God's grace attractive in every way* (Titus 2:10–11). We can extend the principle to leadership. We too help people live as mature disciples by making Jesus look great through everything we do.

> **To consider:**
> Pause for a moment:
>
> - How do you feel you are doing personally at making Jesus seem great to those around you?

- List some of the areas of church life in which you have responsibility. How do you go about making Jesus look great in each area?
- Will people pick up from you that you think that having Jesus gives you the hope of glory?
- How do you feel you are doing at this as a church? Explain your answer.
- If you aren't currently a leader, consider some areas of church life and how they could better be used to make Jesus look great. Perhaps you could encourage your leaders with some of your ideas.

Pointing away from ourselves, towards Jesus

Paul gives a very clear summary of how Christians grow spiritually:

> We are not like Moses, who would put a veil over his face to keep the Israelites from gazing at it while the radiance was fading away. But their minds were made dull, for to this day the same veil remains when the old covenant is read. It has not been removed, because only in Christ is it taken away. Even to this day when Moses is read, a veil covers their hearts. But whenever anyone turns to the Lord, the veil is taken away. Now the Lord is the Spirit, and where the Spirit of the Lord is, there is freedom. And we, who with unveiled faces all reflect the Lord's glory, are being transformed into his likeness with ever-increasing glory, which comes from the Lord, who is the Spirit. (2 Corinthians 3:13–18)

These verses describe the very centre of spiritual leadership. In the Old Testament, people couldn't gaze on God's glory.

They had to be shielded, even from the intense afterglow on Moses face, when he had been with God. However, when we become Christians, the shield can be taken away, so we can look. When we look, says Paul, we reflect God's glory. We start to glow with it, just like Moses did. More than that, as God's glory starts to saturate us, it also transforms us. The more we gaze, the more the Holy Spirit makes our character more and more like Jesus' glorious character.

If we are transformed by the Holy Spirit as we gaze on the glory of God, then the job of leaders is to hold up God's glorious good news so that people can see it, hear it and consider it, in all its technicolour beauty. Our job is not to produce the transformation – the Holy Spirit does that – but to show every magnificent thing about Jesus, as clearly as we can, so that people marvel at him and find him amazing. Leadership is not only *for* the glory of God, it also flows *from* the glory of God. (Always be suspicious of leaders who point to themselves, talk about themselves, or like to give lots of examples in which they are the hero.)

Our character speaks as loudly as our words – or louder

Yesterday two old friends came to see me, bringing their toddler with them. The family likeness was instantly obvious – she has her dad's face! When people start to focus their concentration, what the Bible evocatively describes as the 'eyes of the heart', on the glory of God, they become more like Jesus. The family likeness becomes more and more visible in us.

If it doesn't, then we need to ask what is wrong. People who have positions of spiritual leadership, but who rarely manifest Jesus-like character, are pretenders. Character either proves we really are leaders for God's glory or else it demonstrates that we are leaders for our own glory. This is why Paul instructs Timothy and Titus in what to look for in good leaders: integrity of heart and character all the way.

Character is the overwhelmingly central factor. This is because God wants people who are *like* him, whose leadership is characterized not so much by their dominant personality and skills, as by their humble servant hearts, kindness, repentance, forgiveness and love.

The world values and admires self-made people, those who got to the top and achieved their ambitions by their own merits. Christian leaders are God-made people. We have nothing to boast in, except what God has done in us. We don't glory in what we have achieved, but in what Jesus has achieved. We are at our happiest not when we are being admired, but when God is being adored and honoured.

For young leaders, this is especially tough. It is the easiest mistake to assume that you get on in spiritual leadership in the same way you get on in worldly leadership: by demonstrating your skills and abilities to be admired by others. Many promising young leaders fall at this hurdle because they develop attitudes that prevent them from being servants, replace love with ambition, and rate competence more highly than prayerfulness.

The older I get, the more I want to ask of any leader or potential leader: 'What is your prayer and worship life like? Is your heart soaked in the Bible? Are you an unashamed worshipper? Do you pray for others? Do you have a soft heart?' We are revealed and laid bare by what we love. I want to know whether or not God possesses a leader's heart. That is the only way that the love and grace of God overflow from us to others. When you see these godly character traits emerging in a person's life, there you may discover an excellent spiritual leader in the making.

I haven't come to be served but to serve

The ultimate expression of the heart of spiritual leadership is seen at the cross of Calvary. At the cross, the drama of servant leadership is played out to the fullest and deepest extent. Finally it became apparent what Jesus had meant when he had told his disciples, 'The Son of Man did not come to be served, but to serve, and to give his life as a ransom for many' (Mark 10:45).

They had been bickering about who was the greatest and trying to twist Jesus' arm into letting them be the biggest leaders. How wrong is it possible to be? Status-oriented leadership is the opposite of Jesus-centred leadership. 'Whoever wants to become great among you must be your servant,' said Jesus. 'And whoever wants to be first must be slave of all' (Mark 10:43–44). He himself took the role of a slave when he washed their feet, and then he gave up absolutely everything in order to rescue people for God.

This, says Jesus, is the greatest glory of God. Hours before the cross he told the disciples, 'The hour has come for the Son of Man to be glorified' (John 12:23). He prayed to the Father: '"It was for this very reason I came to this hour. Father, glorify your name!" Then a voice came from heaven, "I have glorified it, and will glorify it again"' (John 12:27–28).

Even as Jesus prays these things, he tells the disciples that cross-centred serving is the mark of real Christians: 'The man who loves his life will lose it, while the man who hates his life in this world will keep it for eternal life. Whoever serves me must follow me; and where I am, my servant also will be. My Father will honour the one who serves me' (John 12:25–26).

Leaders lay down their lives in order to help others make progress in God and enjoy him. We willingly go the way of the cross, setting aside our own desires, so that Christ is formed in the hearts of those we lead. We are overjoyed when the latter are full of faith, standing securely on God's truth and exploding with God-honouring joy.

Spiritual leadership is so much greater than leading services and organizing activities. It is so much bigger than merely teaching and training people. We willingly throw away our lives in order to help others participate with God in growing his kingdom. And so our investment in others is fundamentally different from that of any other kind of leadership in the world. Leaders develop people's souls. Or, as Paul puts it, we work with them for their joy in God.

> **To consider:**
>
> - Who takes an active, personal interest in your progress and joy in God? If you don't have anyone at present, who could you ask?
> - Who do you encourage in this way? If you aren't currently encouraging anyone, write down one or two names, and start to pray about how you could make a start.
> - If you haven't already done so, work through 'Growing in leadership – Practical review exercise' in appendix 2 to help you consider the next steps you can take to grow as a spiritual leader.
> - Thank God that Jesus served you by giving up everything so that you can belong to God's family.

AFTERWORD: A VISION FOR LIFELONG LEARNING

By Tim Chester

I want to invite you to dream with me, to dream of what future training for leadership within your local church could look like.

The great majority of elders, home group leaders, evangelists or children's workers will never attend a residential college. The message of this book is that they don't have to.

It is striking that this is not how the Lord of the church trained the first leaders of the church. Jesus did not send the disciples away to college. He invited them to accompany him on his mission. They were prepared for leadership by walking along the road with him, by observing his ministry, by discussing what they saw. It was the same with the apostle Paul. He himself was probably well educated (Acts 22:3), though he counted this worthless compared with the knowledge he gained in the gospel (Philippians 3:4–8). Paul trained others for leadership like Jesus, by inviting people to accompany him on his mission.

'The things you have heard me say in the presence of many witnesses entrust to reliable men who will also be qualified to teach others' (2 Timothy 2:2). When Paul gives this charge to Timothy he is not talking to the principal of a theological college, but to the leader of a local church.

We may have to revise our image of a leader and the qualifications they need. A leader is not someone with a theology degree. According to 1 Timothy 3, they need to be someone with a godly and exemplary character, someone who can apply God's Word to people's lives, someone who has proven themselves able to lead their family. In-church training will always be viewed as second-class if we continue to believe that 'proper' leaders are those who have gone to Bible college. It's not that no-one should ever undertake residential training, but if this is given a privileged status, then we will continue to have a two-tier view of leadership.

Yes, we need leaders who have a good grasp of sound doctrine. Marcus and I are not advocating anything less. But we need more than this from future leaders. We also need leaders throughout all levels of church life who can communicate well, lead well, pastor well. Too often graduates preach sermons that are orthodox, but which fail to animate hearts or speak to lives. Too often graduates know their Reformation history, but are ill-equipped to lead the body of Christ through change. Too often they know how to speak of Christ in the classroom, but not how to speak of Christ in the pub. Above all we need leaders who love Jesus deeply, who are passionate about his glory, who know the joy of grace, who embody godliness, who find their identity in Christ. Residential training is by no means a guarantee of this.

So let us dream together.

Church-based theological education

We need to provide people with a robust theological education in the context of the leadership roles that they exercise within the local church. This means that theology and mission should always be closely integrated. It also means that training can be accessible and affordable.

Students of our Porterbrook Institute, who are all firmly rooted in local churches in which they exercise a variety of leadership roles, speak again and again of how study material speaks directly and practically into their leadership. And it is a joy to see them bringing the questions that leadership raises to the theological topics we are exploring. On-the-ground, in-church, theological training can provide just as viable a gateway to lifelong leadership learning and growth as residential training models.

Lifelong learning communities

Will training combined with ministry fully equip leaders for a life of ministry? Probably not, not on its own. But then residential colleges do not fully equip people either. We should view either option as a gateway to lifelong learning. It should provide the knowledge and skills that enable people to continue to develop their theological understanding and reflection on practice.

Marcus and I are both convinced, then, that in-church theological education is a good gateway to lifelong learning. Subsequently, we need to provide ongoing training. Leaders need to feel part of a learning community. The Porterbrook Institute, for example, has a programme that enables those who have completed such an education to continue learning through three seminar days each year, and the opportunity to attend taught study days. It is an easily replicable model.

This lifelong learning community also provides a pool for future in-church leader trainers who can be supported to undertake advanced studies. Their potential can be identified through their participation in the learning community, coupled with their week-in, week-out involvement in leadership. They will not be career academics, but gospel-centred leaders in churches with the character and ability to train future generations.

Lifelong support communities

As Marcus has highlighted, too many full-time church leaders do not survive long in leadership. We need to encourage full-timers to find support from within their churches rather than holding themselves at a professional distance. They will need in turn to facilitate similar ongoing nurture and support for leaders at every level. We also need to encourage leaders to find support from their peers through support groups and conferences that not only inform the mind, but affect the heart, like Living Leadership's Pastoral Refreshment Conference. A cohort of junior leaders that are learning together can readily be shaped into support groups or fraternals that provide mutual encouragement.

Marcus and I are part of such a support group that meets twice a year. Our time together typically includes papers for discussion, an extended opportunity to pray for one another, times of corporate worship, an evening in a restaurant, plus plenty of informal time. Having met together for over fifteen years, a strong sense of comradeship has grown up. We have shared in one another's highs and lows, with the group at times being an oasis in difficult periods.

Mentoring and discipleship

The heartbeat of this book is that the task of growing leaders is not the same as preparing good up-front speakers or academics who can do theology. First and foremost, we are preparing disciples. The advantage of church-based training is that people can be discipled in the context of the local church. They can be coached as leaders, their skills can be developed in real-life applications, and above all their relationship with Christ can be nurtured.

Existing leaders need a vision for this kind of mentoring. We may not be able to provide all the theological input young leaders need, but we can disciple and coach them. Some of us will have experienced this ourselves and know what to do. Others will need some training to be leader-disciplers.

Ben is a church worker in a small church in a former mining area. His church currently has no elders. He has much promise, but he is young. He needs someone to disciple and coach him. So once a week, he comes over to our congregation, to talk through his walk with God, his ministry within the church, and to observe what is happening in our context.

This is a great ministry that retired church leaders can participate in. Not everyone comes from a congregation where older leaders are present. In this context, we need to develop a network of mentors who can support young leaders.

Training for training by training

We need to develop a vibrant culture of training, not just for elders, deacons and PCC members, but for home group leaders, Sunday school leaders, youth group leaders. Future church leaders need to have a vision for training, and the best way to do that is to get them involved in training: training them to train by getting them training others! Every aspiring leader should be required to train others as part of their development.

Not every institution or organization needs to provide every aspect in this vision. We can have a mixed economy in which different people provide different aspects of the picture. The important point is that the local church is at the centre.

We pray that the day when churches think that the only way to train leaders is by sending them somewhere else, taking no responsibility themselves, will soon come to an end. We long for the day when every church grasps the crucial importance of releasing a portion of their leaders' time to train and disciple new leaders.

When we look back with the eyes of history, we may wonder why we ever thought it was a good idea to do anything else.

Tim Chester
Porterbrook Institute, 2010

APPENDIX 1: GROWING IN GOD – SPIRITUAL REVIEW QUESTIONS

The following are intended to highlight areas in which you can take practical steps to grow as a Christian. The questions aren't intended to make you feel in any way guilty or depressed, if you feel that the answers aren't what you would like them to be.

For each of the following areas of your spiritual life, try to sum up:

- How have you grown in the past year: lots, some, a bit or not at all?
- If you identify that you have been growing in maturity, what helped you to do so?
- Which one or two main areas would you most like to grow in?
- What practical steps could you take to grow in these areas?

A. Do I have a growing desire for God?

- How is my relationship with the Father?
- Am I aware of living by the Holy Spirit?
- Is my experience of God's grace fresh and current?
- Is my desire for God intensifying or declining at present?

B. Am I actively pursuing Christlikeness?

- Am I aware of the fruit of the Spirit in my life?
- How much would my friends say my life is characterized by forgiveness, kindness, repentance and servanthood?
- Would people say that joy in God is an obvious feature of my life?

C. Am I growing in spiritual beliefs and attitudes?

- Is my appreciation of the cross growing? Or is it the same as it was five years ago?
- Would I say that Jesus has first place in my life?
- How willing am I to surrender things that are important to me to Jesus?
- What are my main spiritual gifts? Would my friends and other leaders agree? Am I currently using them to serve God and others?
- Do I consider the Bible to have authority over me?
- Do I regularly pray to God for guidance?
- Do I pray for opportunities to share Jesus with others?

D. How are my personal spiritual practices?

- Do I take time to adore God?
- Am I regularly reflecting on the Bible and applying it to my life?
- Is my prayer life growing or in decline?
- How would I describe my worship life?
- Am I serving in my area of passion and giftedness?
- Am I using my time and money in God-honouring ways?

E. What opportunities do I have to receive personal spiritual investment from others?

- Do I have any deep spiritual friendships with people who want to help me grow?
- If not, would I like some? (If not, why not?)
- Are any of these friendships secure enough so that I can talk about my patterns of sin?
- Do those friends feel able to speak truth into my life?

APPENDIX 2: GROWING IN LEADERSHIP – PRACTICAL REVIEW EXERCISE

Make a note of what you currently do in the following areas. At the end of the exercise you might want to jot down any areas for development.

Discipling others for their spiritual growth

- Encouraging people to grow in love for God
- Helping others identify their spiritual gifts and find appropriate ways to use them
- Helping others grow in spiritual disciplines such as worship, prayer, giving or fasting
- Knowing how to help people who have stalled spiritually

Building Bible-centred prayerful living

- Helping people know how to feed themselves from God's Word rather than being passive receivers from others
- Helping people know how to apply what the Bible says to their lives

Building a community of depth

- Building openness, honesty and willingness to share struggles as well as joys between Christians
- Understanding how to help groups (for example, house groups or the choir) interact positively and encourage one another
- Encouraging individuals and groups within the church to serve the church as a whole

Helping others have a vision for growing God's kingdom

- Helping others understand and vocalize the vision and purpose of a local church and their place within it
- Helping people grasp how they can participate in God's big purposes to save more and more people
- Helping people know how to witness to, and disciple, others so that they make progress in their faith and discover joy in God

APPENDIX 3: ELEMENTS TO INCLUDE IN A LEADER-TRAINING COURSE IN YOUR CHURCH

The purpose of offering training for leaders is to support their continued growth and, thereby, the spiritual vitality of the church. When approached with the right aims, training can provide far more than simply helping people acquire new skills. Other components include:

- Providing a group environment for mutual encouragement, as leaders pray, learn and grow together
- Helping leaders sustain shared values, common goals, mutual strategy and a commitment to being a team together at the heart of church life
- Undergirding leaders' skills by providing appropriate resources
- Thanking leaders and honouring their service, recognizing the vital contribution they bring to building up God's people
- Developing a context where it is normal for embryonic new leaders to grow

Right at the top of my list is the need to disciple leaders for their own spiritual formation. It is critical to consider this separately from training in specific skills or competencies, because the way you do each differs. One is a long-term, life-on-life investment. The other can be done in a training day or evening.

Many churches and most leaders live with severe pressures on their time. This makes it attractive to want to deliver skills training rather than discipling for spiritual growth because it is much less time-intensive. If you have the resources only to do the former but not the latter, then you need to bear in mind that just because you have put on some training doesn't necessarily mean that those you have trained are guaranteed to be growing as Christians.

Discipling for spiritual growth

When we disciple leaders, the aim is to help a Christian (who happens to be a leader, but that is comparatively unimportant) grow in Christ. We want to see Christ being formed in their hearts through faith, so that they live and lead as a wholehearted disciple.

There are no quick fixes. If you want to disciple someone, he or she is going to require a good-sized chunk of your life. It is worth it, however, because discipleship is the foundation that subsequently ensures that training in skills and competencies falls into spiritually fertile soil.

So how do we help others grow? Here are some of the main elements I would include:

- How to live their life (and exercise their leadership) based on a daily appreciation of justification and God's amazing grace
- How being adopted as children of God should shape character, goals and relationships

- How prayer and worship life are central to their joy in God (this is core to my understanding of how to stay spiritually fresh as a leader)
- How increasingly Christlike leaders will want to outdo everyone else in love, humility, repentance, forgiveness and kindness; leadership integrity is a result of Christlike character
- What exhibiting the Galatians 5 fruit of the Holy Spirit means in practice in our lives

It stands to reason that we cannot help others if we aren't committed to growing in these things ourselves. We cannot be good leaders unless we are good followers. Indeed the whole point of training others in skills is so that they will use them to disciple other people.

There is lots of really helpful material for use in discipling leaders. Among the best are the *Sonship* and *Gospel Transformation* courses by the World Harvest Mission (www.whm.org). The *Sonship* course in particular has been written to disciple leaders. Many leaders with whom I have used it have found it deeply beneficial.

Training in leadership skills

Shorter training sessions in focused skills and areas of competence are also extremely helpful. We should want every leader in our churches to be better equipped in five years' time than they are now.

There are some specialisms in which a small minority of leaders need expertise, but which are unnecessary for most. Examples might include such things as developing a child safety policy or understanding the legal framework within which charity trustees operate. But there are other areas of practical servanthood in which all leaders constantly need to grow, whether they are being trained for the first time, or being encouraged and helped for the hundredth. Here are seven main elements which you could include in such training, along with some possible subjects:

1. Understanding the core of spiritual leadership and how to maintain a fresh walk with God as a leader
2. How to disciple others and help them live God-centred lives, increasingly full of faith:
    i) Working with others for their progress and joy
    ii) Helping others have a passion to grow in spiritual maturity
    iii) Helping others develop healthy spiritual friendships and accountabilities
    iv) Encouraging one another to love and do good deeds
    v) Building a discipleship mentality in a small group
    vi) Helping people discover and develop their spiritual gifts and ministry for God
3. Being part of a team for God's glory:
    i) Leading teams, including home groups
    ii) Facilitating fellowship and in-depth relationships
    iii) Understanding different leadership styles
    iv) Leadership and loyalty – how to respond when you disagree with other church leaders
4. Growing Bible-centred believers:
    i) How to read and understand the Bible
    ii) How to prepare and lead effective, well-applied Bible discussions
    iii) Growing beyond study to absorbing, applying, praying, obeying and worshipping

5. Building community:
    i) Developing, communicating and leading from vision
    ii) Handling difference and change
    iii) Helping new people understand how the church works
    iv) Leading a good preaching and worship meeting
    v) Leading corporate prayer
    vi) Helping others participate in the church's evangelism and outreach
    vii) Dealing with incompatible requests and demands in church life
    viii) Making wise, gospel-centred decisions
    ix) Confronting sin
    x) Troubleshooting in difficult church relationships
    xi) Handling discouragement, disappointment and temptation
6. Growing in pastoring:
    i) Encouraging those who are suffering
    ii) Helping those struggling with sin
    iii) Helping those struggling with doubt
    iv) Knowing your limits and where to get help
7. Being a leader-maker

The list could go on. In deciding which elements to select for a leaders' training programme, you might like to consider which areas you think you currently develop well in and which you omit, and why.

APPENDIX 4: LEADERSHIP-KILLERS

Here, in no particular order, is the list of spiritual-leadership killers mentioned in chapter 9. I have personally come across instances of all of these – often more than once – in the past five years. Some of these discouragements are more common among full-time leaders, but many are echoed by leaders at all levels of church life.

Pressures on family and friendships

- People are happy for me and my family to make sacrifices that they aren't prepared to make. People think I can live on thin air. The pay and conditions are terrible. This gets harder and harder, the older I get, especially as they all have houses to live in, but have never paid me enough to get on the property ladder or to buy a house when I retire.
- People think there should be no line between personal life and church life. Lack of boundaries damages my family life by making my family public property. My children have to be the best behaved in the church or it reflects badly on me.
- The church has inappropriate expectations of the role my spouse should play.

- I am expected to not have any friends among those I lead in order to avoid favouritism. I am lonely.

Feeling devalued

- My work skills are trivialized. Everyone else has a view on how I should do the job, but it would be inconceivable for me to tell them how to do theirs.
- There is no sense of honouring and obeying leaders, as the Bible teaches. There is a fear that if people do so, then leaders will fall into the trap of needing to be adulated. The congregation think that not honouring leaders keeps them humble.
- I connect what I do and who I am very closely. When what I do is challenged, resisted or fails, my personal sense of self-worth is damaged.
- I am regularly accused of not delivering what people want.
- My congregation compare me to their favourite preacher on the internet or The God Channel. Or to the previous person in the job, or to their favourite historical preacher – always unfavourably.
- A large percentage of congregation members think the role of leaders is simply to run all their favourite activities.

Feeling unable to lead

- People won't follow my leadership, or they actively resist me.
- I have multiple competing interest groups in the church, with incompatible wishes and demands.
- My congregation is full of passive receivers and consumers. They expect me to do everything while they don't do anything.

- The church is made up of people who may be believers, but for all the difference it seems to make in their lives they might as well be atheists. The only functional difference is that they attend church on a Sunday.
- A large percentage of people are long-term spiritually stalled and do not wish to leave the rut they run in. Everything I do to encourage them to take new steps is resisted.
- Whenever I face down opposition, it only ever gets worse. To try to wear me down people will query procedures, then my wisdom, then my integrity, then suggest that I have hidden motives, then threaten to split the church, then write me hateful letters.

Feeling the job is too big for me

- The job is simply too big for me. I am exhausted all the time. I reach the limit of my time and abilities long before I reach the limit of people's expectations.
- I am spiritually drained.
- I feel out of control, spinning too many plates.
- I don't have an evaluative process or any other way to know whether I am doing the right things as a spiritual leader.
- I am judged exclusively by visible work. Therefore I am tempted to squeeze out my personal devotional life.

Feeling spiritually isolated

- I can't talk to anyone about doubt or sin without losing my job. I am the only person in the church whose job depends on an appearance of sinlessness.

- I am expected to take responsibility for everyone else's spiritual growth and health. No-one expects to take responsibility for mine.
- I see two different stories: the church as it ought to be and as it really is; me as I ought to be and as I really am. Therefore I have to live behind a mask all the time, so that nobody really knows me. My church expects pretence and a veil of superficiality.
- I can't express fears, frustrations or sins to a denominational supervisor because they have power over possible future ministry opportunities.
- I try to develop structures such as home groups for everyone else's spiritual help. However, I am the only person who is expected to not participate as my presence would intimidate a group.
- Whenever I lead worship, I don't really get to worship myself. I regularly teach others but don't have opportunities to be taught myself.

FURTHER READING

There are hundreds of books on Christian leadership. Here is a small selection of accessible ones that I have found valuable and keep on my shelf for regular reference.

Understanding leadership

- Richard Baxter, *The Reformed Pastor* (1665 – the original classic!).
- Derek Tidball, *Builders and Fools: Leadership the Bible Way* (IVP, 1999).
- Peter White, *The Effective Pastor: Get the Tools to Upgrade Your Ministry* (Mentor, 2002).
- Walter C. Wright, *Relational Leadership* (Paternoster, 2000).

Leadership character

- Jonathan Lamb, *Integrity: Leading with God Watching* (IVP, 2006).

Growing as a leader

- Colin Buckland, *Freedom to Lead: Healthy Leaders Grow Healthy Churches* (CWR, 2006).

- Bill Hybels, *Courageous Leadership* (Zondervan, 2002).
- James Lawrence, *Growing Leaders: Reflections on Leadership, Life and Jesus* (CPAS, 2004).
- John Piper, *Brothers, We Are Not Professionals: A Plea to Pastors for Radical Ministry* (Mentor, 2003).

Surviving as a leader

- Peter Brain, *Going the Distance: How to Stay Fit for a Lifetime of Ministry* (Matthias Media, 2004).
- Kent and Barbara Hughes, *Liberating Ministry from the Success Syndrome* (Crossway Books, 2008).
- James Taylor, *Pastors Under Pressure* (Day One, 2004).

Leadership wisdom

- Barbara Miller Juliani (ed.), *The Heart of a Servant Leader: Letters from Jack Miller* (R&R Publishing, 2004). If you only ever buy and read one book on this list, get this one. It's worth its weight in gold.
- Eugene Peterson, *Working the Angles: The Shape of Pastoral Integrity* (Eerdmans, 1993).
- Eugene Peterson, *Under the Unpredictable Plant: An Exploration in Vocational Holiness* (Eerdmans, 1994).

Leadership practicalities

- Harold Rowdon (ed.), *Church Leaders Handbook* (Paternoster, 2002).
- Neil Summerton, *A Noble Task: Eldership and Ministry in the Local Church* (Paternoster, 1994).
- Rick Warren, *The Purpose Driven Church: Growth without Compromising Your Message and Mission* (Zondervan, 1995).

WHAT IS LIVING LEADERSHIP?

Living Leadership
Training and Sustaining Biblical Leaders

Living Leadership is a dynamic and growing network of leaders who are committed to training and sustaining leaders for God's glory. We believe that identifying, training, developing and sustaining leaders is a key task for churches in every generation, and especially critical at the current time.

We long to see leaders developed who make a difference for Christ in the local and global church. We believe that training, development and ongoing nurture of life, soul and skills should be easily available and financially accessible for all leaders and their spouses.

Living Leadership is achieving this goal through three strands of initiatives:

- Helping embryonic and junior leaders grow as grace-filled servants
- Nurturing, developing, sustaining and caring for current leaders and spouses
- Providing training opportunities for volunteer leaders – elders, deacons, PCC members, house group leaders, etc. – through local church training events

To find out more and to download our growing selection of free leaders' resources, please visit our website:

www.livingleadership.org.

Commendations for Living Leadership

Teaching from Living Leadership has laid a foundation for the Bible and Culture course at Schloss Mittersill. When they teach on grace they do it with great grace.
Dr Christian Bensel, Director of Bible and Culture

I'm excited about the work that Living Leadership is doing. And I'm excited about the values that shape that work – a generous unity in Christ, a focus on the heart as well as the head and fostering the joy of grace.
Tim Chester, pastor and author

Living Leadership is a very timely initiative. Pastoral encouragement, spiritual sustenance and sustaining grace are often neglected priorities for Christian leaders, but they are absolutely essential in today's hazardous environment. I am delighted to see such a network being launched, and support it wholeheartedly.
Jonathan Lamb, Director of Langham Preaching, Chairman of the Keswick Convention, IFES former Associate General Secretary

The teaching week on Christian leadership was a great balance of practical and theological rigour. It was both a blessing and a challenge. All the boys thought it was magic!
MA student, Wales Evangelical School of Theology

Living Leadership's Pastoral Refreshment Conference proved to be one of the best gatherings I have been to in years. It is unique and a blessing. It is billed as 'enjoying God, receiving refreshment and being encouraged', and we had all three in bucketloads!
Melvin Tinker, vicar, St John's Newland, Hull

NOTES

Chapter 3 Clear, dig and nurture
1 The Bible has hundreds of references to leadership, lists of the character qualities and skills of leaders, and narrative accounts of what leaders do.
2 Here are some key Bible passages you might like to look up: Matthew 28:16–20; Acts 20:28; Ephesians 3:7 – 4:13; 1 Timothy 3; 1 Peter 2:9–10.

Chapter 4 Developing yourself as a spiritual leader
1 Howard Guinness, *Sacrifice* (Young Life by permission of IVP, 1989), p. 71f.

Chapter 6 Caring for yourself as a leader
1 'A Sermon (No. 97) delivered on Sabbath Morning, August 17, 1856, by the REV. C. H. Spurgeon at New Park Street Chapel, Southwark', http://www.spurgeon.org/sermons/0097.htm.

Chapter 7 You could be a leader-maker
1 This isn't original to me. I picked it up from the teaching of Colin Buckland. All leaders would benefit greatly from his books on leadership.

Chapter 8 Look out – There's a cliff!

1 Quoted in Peter Brain, *Going the Distance: How to Stay Fit for a Lifetime of Ministry* (Matthias Media, 2004), p. 16.

Chapter 9 How to love and encourage spiritual leaders

1 Eugene Peterson, *Under the Unpredictable Plant: An Exploration in Vocational Holiness* (Eerdmans, 1994), p. 2.
2 Sermon on Hebrews 13:17, 12 October 1997, www.desiringgod.org.
3 As a rule of thumb, most full-time church leaders work upwards of sixty hours a week, and many work over seventy. A large percentage indicate that they never have a completely uninterrupted day off. Most meet the law of diminishing returns at around fifty to fifty-five hours, after which additional work ceases to be good work, due to tiredness.
4 Gordon MacDonald, *Restoring Your Spiritual Passion* (Highland, 1986), p. 73ff.

Chapter 10 Let your leaders lead

1 Derek Tidball, *Builders and Fools: Leadership the Bible Way* (IVP, 1999), p. 103f.
2 Ibid. p. 111f.